MW00936520

WORDS AND SEEDS

The Power Behind Your Words

Mae Archila

WestBow Press books may be ordered through booksellers or by contacting:

WestBow Press
A Division of Thomas Nelson
1663 Liberty Drive
Bloomington, IN 47403
www.westbowpress.com
1-(866) 928-1240

cover image designed by Carolina Karim

ISBN: 978-1-4497-0897-9 (sc)
ISBN: 978-1-4497-0896-2 (e)

Library of Congress Control Number: 2010943350

Printed in the United States of America

WestBow Press rev. date: 4/11/2011

Dedication

I am eternally grateful to God, who has fashioned me as a writer, enabling me, to be a part of reaching the world with life.

I dedicate this book to Oscar, my loving husband, and to our three wonderful children; Mark, Javier and Carolina.

Acknowledgments

I would like to thank and acknowledge some wonderful people who helped in getting this manuscript to become a reality. Without their encouragement, prayers, and support this book might not have been in your hands today.

My wonderful husband, Oscar, diligently stood by me through many hours and days, listening as I read and re-read to him. His prayers and desire for me to write this book were at times stronger than mine. He kept me inspired and motivated.

Our beautiful daughter, Carolina, so willingly sowed her time and talent in designing the cover.

Our two sons, Mark and Javier, were a tremendous help, their support and love came with unspeakable joy.

Our very best friends Johan and Veronique, never left my side in prayer and encouragement. Our many *get-a-ways* help clear my mind and re-adjust my focus.

A dear friend of mine, Alean Ford, an author herself, inspired me, prayed for me and with me. Her inspiration kept me on track as she spent many hours, days, and months editing for me.

A very special man, Bishop W. W. Thomas, gave me my first book on the power of words called, *Fruit of the Lips* by Don

Hughes, which inspired me to write this book. Before he went home to be with the Lord, he gave me his blessing for this book.

I am forever grateful to the wonderful staff at West Bow Press for all their valuable time poured into this book.

Foreword

"Words" are so powerful that Our Creator, God Almighty used them: *"In the beginning God created..."* (Genesis 1:1).

By what means did God create? By speaking His "Word." He spoke, *"Let there be...."* He created the entire earth and universe with *words*.

Jesus also taught many lessons and used parables to teach His disciples about the *power of words*, the importance of planting good seed in good soil, and expecting a great and lasting harvest. What kinds of *words* and *seeds* are you planting daily in your heart and in others? Remember: *"Life and death are in the power of the tongue, and whatever we sow that, will we also reap."*

God is a faith God, and He is touching and planting His faith *words* and *seeds* of greatness in our hearts, and yet what are we doing that is really touching His heart?

Words and Seeds will uplift, encourage, and broaden your horizons helping you to accomplish all you were meant to be.

The message of this book will challenge you to examine the *words* and *seeds* that you plant daily in the hearts and minds of children and others around you. You too, must lay a strong foundation of the *Word*, which Mae Archila has done in her own personal experiences and revelation that God has given her. Are you desperate to go much deeper into the things of God, and complete the good work that He has begun in you? If the answer is *yes* then this book is for you!

I am honored to have the privilege of knowing and working with Mae Archila. I love and respect her walk with God! Her greatest desire is to please God through sharing her gifts, talents and resources with others in need whether at home or around the world.

Mae Archila is a woman of God with wisdom, integrity, and godly principles, who loves and respects her husband and children. Mae has a heart to see the Body of Christ, the church, come into a deeper intimacy with Jesus through prayer, faith, and action from the truth of the *spoken word* and the *written Word of God!*

Alean M. Ford
Author of: *Look Up and Live*
Poems from the Heart
What I Need to Know as a Christian
Tell Them That I Love Them!

Contents

Introduction

Sticks and Stones

"Sticks and stones may break my bones,
but words will never hurt me!"

Many of us at some time have heard this child's quote: "Sticks and stones *may* break my bones,..." I'm sure we'd all agree that this part of the quote is definitely true, but it was the second part of the verse that had always troubled me: "...but words will never hurt me." Even as a child, I knew, without a doubt, *words did hurt!*

During my early years, I remember words having been the source of much of my frustration. I still recall one instance in elementary school during recess when some annoying bullies had been picking on me and my friend. We tried to ignore them, but even walking away didn't stop their use of cruel words. In defense, I turned around and faced them yelling out with boldness and rage, *"Sticks and stones may break my bones, but words will never hurt me!"* Well, I really don't know if it was the tone of my voice, or the fact that I stood up to them that made them stop. Nevertheless, all day long and into the week I could still feel the sting of their words, which had penetrated deep within my heart. The bottom line was that their words *did* hurt.

I'm sure, if you think back, you too could recall such an event. Maybe the harmful words came from a parent, teacher, a person of authority or maybe even from a bully. In any case, those words have traveled with you through life only to appear at the worst of times. In this book, we will learn that words are so powerful that when negatively spoken, they can undermine our self-esteem, attack our true being or the ridicule they cause can even affect our future. On the other hand, positive words can uplift, encourage, and broaden our horizons helping us to accomplish all we were meant to be.

During my search for a title for this book a song came to me in a dream. The song was written by Herb Newman called, "The Birds and the Bees." If you remember this catchy tune, hum along with me.

***"Let me tell ya 'bout the Birds and the Bees,
and the Flowers and the Trees, and the Moon
up above, and a thing called Love."***

The following morning I was unable to shake this song out of my head. It was then that the six chapters of this book were birthed. Let *me* tell you about the *Words* and the *Seeds,* and the *Flowers* and the *Trees,* and the *Moon* up above, and a thing called *Love.* The original song was referring to the facts of life, but since most of us already know about the birds and the bees, I'd like to introduce *Words* and *Seeds* as facts of life most essential and valuable to us all.

"Fact" is known to be the realness and the truth of something, therefore, this book refers to the realness and the truth of life, and how our *words* can affect it.

In this book we will learn *facts* and *truths* about our lives based on the power behind the words spoken to us or by us, whether good or bad. With this information we can begin to check our speech before we let out a word to those around us. First and foremost, we will be able to think back on what we have said, and what has been said to us realizing how our lives have been affected today. In reading this book, I am convinced that we can actually become better persons.

***The Words We Leave Behind, Especially Those Spoken
Will Be A Lasting Picture Of Who We Are.***

CHAPTER ONE

Words

Freedom of Speech

As far back as 1789, our forefathers must have been thinking about the power of words, because they had a really good idea—they established the *Bill of Rights.* While reading the restrictions of the "Ten Amendments", I was impressed with the "First Amendment" relating to *free speech.* (Note: For easier reading, I added bold to some words.)

"The First Amendment, relating to religion, free speech, right of assembly and petition, debars Congress from establishing a religion or prohibiting free exercise of religion, ***or abridging the freedom of speech*** *or of the press, or the right of the people peaceably to assemble and to petition the government for a redress of grievances."*

Was I reading this right? Does this convey that Congress is prevented from depriving the people of speaking freely? Strictly speaking, this is a fair and legitimate law for us all.

The center and lower part of the second paragraph reads, "*. . . but freedom of speech and of the press does not permit the publication of libels, blasphemous or other indecent articles, or other publications injurious to moral or private reputation. A publisher is subject to punishment for contempt if his articles tend to obstruct the administration of justice.*

The right of free speech does not give immunity for every possible use of language."

Do we legally have the freedom to say whatever we feel like saying even if it is wrong? No, not legally. Nevertheless, it is happening all around us! We can do so much with what is at our disposal, and *words* are ours to use freely. If used properly, we have a freedom that is backed up by the Constitution. How cool is that!

If everyone watched what they said and did, we wouldn't have to concern ourselves with trying to protect little ears and little eyes and even our mouths—but we do. It is a tough job, and someone has to do it. If we are all willing to change our way of speaking and apply what we learn, can you imagine how we could actually start changing the world one *word* at a time?

Change is vital to our survival. Waiting for perfect conditions will mean inactivity. This practical insight is especially applicable to our use of *words*. It should be happening now. The greatest of all mistakes is to do nothing because you think you can only do a little. Imagine every single person doing a little. It's obvious that all around us, wherever we go, there are just down-right, mean people who don't have any desire to help, but for most of us who do want to make a difference in this world, it will require *change*. Other than voting and participating in methods and programs to help the sick, the poor, the young, the animals, and even the ozone, there are still many things to be done which may require further learning. We should always be ready and willing to learn in spite of age or position, never once thinking that we already know it all regardless how ingenious we naturally are. Remember, *change* requires us to keep up and keep moving forward.

Children and grandchildren are great in keeping us updated on new technology. When I received my Nintendo DS (handheld game console) as a gift from my grandchildren, it provided me with many fun challenges and opportunities. Life should be as such.

Mariana Valverde wrote, *"It is said that one book does not change the world, and that is true. But what does change the world?"* She goes on, *"A fast or slow process, depending on the situation, but always incessant, and with a thousand dimensions. The written word is one of them, and not merely an auxiliary wheel."* (This quote is not referring to the Bible as the written word). Personally, I believe there is one other truth of being the number one process that can change the world over and above the written *word*, and that is the spoken *word*. Teachers who love to read out loud are actually bringing the written word into action.

The written word is an action ready to happen, and the spoken word is the action in progress.

In the five years teaching cute little kindergarteners, I learned many valuable and precious lessons including songs. My cuties had a favorite song, and it went something like this: *"Be careful little eyes what you see, be careful little ears what you hear..."* and so forth. This not only was a cute little song, but it carried a valuable message with it. It is easy for anyone to believe that life through the eyes of a child is unraveled. Their unlived life is wrapped up innocence, and purity of mind is natural to them. Our child's first lessons and first training begins at home. Change begins to take place. Even an adult begins to change once a child is in the picture. No training or education of our children should be left entirely to a teacher. Yes, there are a lot of great teachers out in the world, and many do over and above their required duty, because they care. Both teacher and parent should understand, without a doubt, that a child is a part of the future, and their training should aim for the best future they can ever have. I believe that the character of a child can be known by the way he acts, whether what he does is right or wrong.

The following points may be helpful in keeping our tongue under control and avoid slips of the lips, especially around our children: Be careful of (1) whom you speak of; (2) whom you speak to; (3) how you speak; (4) when you speak; (5) where you speak, and (6) why you speak.

Though most of what you have read so far may sound somewhat childish, wouldn't you say it has great truth? Most everything that is written or done for children has come from an adult. I am a firm believer that great truths, insight, and wisdom and knowledge are imparted to us by God; so if *He can get it to us, then He can get it through us to others.* In order to change our world, we must let God get the good stuff in us so He can work through us into the lives of others. The greatness within us was meant to be shared, and through our own *words* we carry great potential to make a difference.

The Power of Words

Once upon a time, there was a beautiful, talented young girl full of life and loved by everyone. In her heart she knew she was destined for greatness. Her dreams and goals for the future were celebrated as she was lavished with an abundance of flourishing, profitable, and favorable words from her family and friends. Later, as a young woman, she made a wrong choice that shattered her dreams. The words full of life once spoken to her diminished all together. Those who once celebrated her no longer supported her. Not even realizing it, she was hearing negative words, words full of disappointment, hopelessness, depression, and even words of discouragement and disrespect. Comments such as, *"What a messed up life you've made of yourself! You will never amount to anything! Now, no one will ever love you. You no longer have value!"* were thrust at her. She believed and lived her dreamless life. After many lonely years she died, and her life died also.

"If you do not live the life you believe, you will believe the life you live." –ZIG ZIGLAR

What captivated my attention about this woman was not that she died, but that her life died also. In looking up the word "life", one single word jumped out at me from its long definition—"energy." We know that life is the present state of existence of anything, so therefore, the absence of life is death, having no energy, nor state of existence, right? To die is to cease living or cease existing, or better yet, to expire. What died, in this woman, was her energy, her dreams, the touch that many should have felt, the love that was to bloom, the functions and activities that were to be performed by merely her existence. Without a doubt, the lifeless *words* spoken over her had caused harm, and damaged her true being. She never encountered the strength or methods to overcome such tragedy. So I understood how death could overcome life by the power of the tongue.

Several years ago, I read a story that truly brings to light the power of *words*. The story is about a little boy whose parents took him to see his grandfather, who was very ill in the hospital. The parents, not knowing whether it was appropriate for the child to see his grandpa in his weakest state of health, asked the child to wait in the lobby until they returned for him. After what seemed hours and hours of waiting, the little boy went off on his own looking for his parents. He continued poking his little head in and out of rooms. The grandpas he saw all seemed to look alike, laying on big white beds with tubes and machines connected to them. Finally, he saw a frail old man lying in bed that fit the memory of his grandpa. He slowly and quietly tiptoed into the room. Still wondering where his parents were, he figured a quick visit would be best. Stepping up next to the big bed, he pushed a chair closer to climb up on Grandpa's side, as he recalled doing when he spent the night two summers ago.

Tenderly he spoke, *"Hi, Grandpa."* Carefully leaning in closer, he said, *"I'm glad I found you. I love you so much, and I really want you to get better so we can spend more summers fishing, and building sailboats and go-carts together."*

Fitting his small warm hand into Grandpa's large cold one he continued, *"Remember when you asked me what I would like to be when I grow up, and I said an astronaut? You said I can be anything I wanted to be if I wanted it bad enough."* His eyes welled up with tears, *"So, what I want is for you to get better, if you want it bad enough. I want you to teach me more smart words so I will know what to do when I grow up. I remember you telling me to watch my words because they are very valuable. Grandpa, I even remember you saying that words are as good as medicine when used right."* He paused to wipe his tears. *"Grandpa, am I using my words right, are they making you feel better?"* He paused as if waiting for grandpa to answer. *"Well, if they are, then I can't wait until you get out of here. Hospitals are for the sick, and soon you will not be sick anymore, right?"* Quickly glancing at the door and back, he concluded, *"I have to go look for Mom and Dad now. I think they're lost. Take care, Grandpa. I'll see you next summer, okay?"*

Gently kissing Grandpa on the cheek, the lively boy jumped off the bed, and ran off to meet up with his parents in the hallway near the waiting lobby. *"Come on son we must go now,"* his father said, *"we'll be back when Grandpa is feeling better, okay?"*

"Okay," he answered without hesitation, and they all left together. A few weeks later, both Grandpas were out of the hospital. The Grandpa whom the little boy had spoken to had been in a coma for months prior to a very special visit from a lively child with life in his words.

"Gentle words cause life and health" (Proverbs 15:4 LV).

Long ago, Rudyard Kipling, a wise man once wrote, *"Words are…the most powerful drug used by mankind."* To me, this means that just like drugs, *words* can heal, but on the same note, overdoses and improper usage can cause great harm and possibly death. Are our *words* pleasing, helping or harming?

"Our words should aim not to please, but to help." -SENECA

This above quote reminds me of the importance of speaking properly to children. As a teacher, I pretty much figured out how moms and dads spoke at home in just listening to their child's manner of speaking. In teaching art, I often heard, *"I can't, my mom (or dad) says I am not an artist."* Sadly, I even heard, *"Dad (or Mom) says I can't draw."* In believing their parents, a child gives up even before trying. Thanks to the many teachers that have found creative methods and *words* to speak to such children helping them to believe in themselves and in what they *can* do. Children are as little sponges ready to absorb it all in, yet so vulnerable—taking our *words* as gold. In general, smaller children idolize their parents and/or teachers seeing the world as a playground—learning as they play. Our *words* should aim to create safety for our children. Children should feel safe and confident in themselves, believing that they are valuable to life. More importantly, every adult can choose to have a major part in any youngster's early life, which in turn allows them the privilege in building a better future through them. We need strong, dedicated parents raising strong, dedicated, law-abiding adults (not children) who are properly loved, and taught. These children, right now, are being transformed into adulthood one step at a time. Every step of their journey is important. We have that honor to be foundation builders in their lives. As future builders, we must settle for nothing less than the best quality of materials used at home and in our families. These adults-in-the-making are our hope for tomorrow. We have the greatest tools to use, and one is the *spoken word.*

An ancient Greek quote says it best:

"A word out of season may mar a whole life."

As a young teenager, I babysat a lot of children, some of which, I considered to be brats. One dictionary defines "brat" as a spoiled child. At one point in my life, I heard that some kids are spoiled well, and yet others are spoiled badly? How can this be? Well, unfortunately, the meaning of *spoil* is not desirable at all when referring to children.

A noun definition of "spoil" means waste or corruption, while the verb definition means to rob, strip, corrupt, damage, destroy, harm, injure, mess up, ruin, wreck…(the list goes on and on). What an awful thing to happen to a child! After reading this bit of information, no parent or grandparent would be in their right mind to ever want to spoil a child! I personally like to pamper my children and my grandchildren. According to folk psychology, one spoils a child by giving in to their whining, letting them have their way, or giving them privileges they haven't earned or deserved. As a result, they may well come to demand special privileges as a matter of right, and may become self-centered, conceited, and selfish. Even an adult may be spoiled in a similar way by getting unaccustomed luxuries, so that he can no longer be content or even appreciate what he had before.

Something else made super sense to me as a young babysitter and as a teacher in my later years: a child's actions and words defined their character or in some cases, their parents' character. In my research and study of children on the playground, in church, in stores, restaurants, parks, classrooms and in many other settings, it became evident that youthful behavior, especially in the child's manner of speaking was most often the result of following adult behavior. A lot of what a small child says or does is natural to them. The mirror image of actions and *words* seen or heard around them are not taken in by them with understanding, especially if it is heard or done around them enough times to consider it natural in their way of thinking. Actually, it is sad to say that at times some adults may behave in the same manner.

Seeing one child on the table eating out of the sugar bowl, and the youngest attempting to climb up for her share, I quickly removed the half empty sugar bowl, only to hear crying, *"I'm going to tell Mommy that you won't let me do that!"*

"Do what, sit on the table and eat sugar?" It took all of me to calmly turn to the five year old sister and asked, *"Do you do this at home and does Mommy let you eat sugar out of the sugar bowl?"*

Her answer without hesitation was, *"Yes,"* I was dumbfounded!

Another time, I was invited to go out to a restaurant with a family and their two small children. Once in the crowded restaurant, it was obvious that the children did not want to be there. They immediately began acting up. I was wrong to think that the two children were trying their hardest to escape, the three year old by wiggling out of the booth and the youngest one out of the highchair. Everyone else in the diner was aware of the one child screaming and the other whining and complaining about her food and not wanting to be there. Though embarrassed, I couldn't help notice the parents ignoring their two children, as they continued to talk among themselves. As the babysitter, I was limited in what I could do at the moment, not to mention being the children's least favorite person there. Even in their throwing food at me and making faces, I understood that their main goal was to get their parent's attention. This was a sure sign that they just wanted Mommy and Daddy. The waitress even limited her service trips to our table. Since the children's improper behavior was not being corrected, they continued as competing with each others' acts of rudeness. Time seem to just linger on and on. I might not have remembered what I ate, but I can definitely recall the grand performance. By this time, I thought maybe the parents were ignoring the children because correcting them would only consume the little bit of time they had to spend together, since they were both working parents. I've heard that sparing the rod spoils the child. Some parents have spared the rod a bit, too, many times. As parents, there will be many times when we must choose to sacrifice our "honey" time just to give them some honey time. My own children knew that no matter where we were, I always carried the rod—my hand. A good spanking at times was what they needed even if it hurt me more.

"Scolding and spanking a child helps him to learn. Left to himself, he brings shame to his mother"
(Proverbs 29:15 LV).

I believe that if we discipline our children they will give us happiness and peace of mind. This is talking about discipline, not punishment.

As parents, we have all grown weary of disciplining our children. Sometimes many of us feel that all we do is nag, scold, and punish and are tempted to give up and let them do whatever they want. Even in thinking that we have ruined every chance for a loving relationship with them, we shouldn't give in. As parents, we need to stand up for what we believe is right, whether our children understand or not. Remember, kind and firm discipline helps them learn, and learning makes them wise.

Constant, loving discipline will ultimately teach them to discipline themselves. As a parent, I found it tough many times, but staying firm brings great rewards. My daughter, once she became an adult, thanked me for how I raised her. She knows now why some parents have to be strict. Though difficult at times, if we all focus on what kind of adults we're aiming to raise it might make it an easier and clearer goal. An adult that understands discipline can teach discipline.

"Discipline" is a training that is expected to produce a specific character or pattern of behavior especially that which is expected to produce moral or mental improvement. Discipline also suggests training by instruction and establishing self-control. In disciplining our children, we must not forget that communication goes hand in hand with correction. We must remember to explain to the child why we have chosen such methods of correction such as spanking, grounding or extra chores. Even children want to know and have the right to know why things happen to them. With open communication, even through their discipline, they will eventually know that we care. Discipline helps them build character, therefore building their future.

"Punishment" is not training. It causes a person pain, loss, or suffering. It also tears down character, therefore tearing down our future. We must be careful in knowing the difference around our children.

Although life moves on and things progressively change, unfortunately most children's behavior still seems a bit weak. To all intents and purposes, children continue behaving bad. My question was, *why*?

It wasn't until I was married and wanted a family that I thought about this again. When my husband had asked me how many children we should have, I answered, *"five"* as if putting in an order. I continued with such assurance, *"And I want them to be well behaved and well-mannered wherever they are, and I want them to know it."* I had a plan!

As our children came into our lives we began to speak good things into them. At different ages they responded to words such as: *"You are such a good boy."*, *"What a good-looking boy you are."*, *"I'm so proud of you."*, *"I liked how you sat there, you were the best kid in the whole room."*, *"That was such a nice thing to say."*, *"You are so smart."*, *"You do such good work."*, *"You make me so happy."*, or even, *"You are so wonderful."* Words with life will get a child to believe in himself and strive to do better each time. In fact, many believe that a sincere compliment is the most effective teaching and motivational method in existence today.

So often, out in public our own children would recognize brats and spoiled children, identifying in them improper behavior. If you speak proper, and act proper in the home, then your children will grow up knowing what is and isn't acceptable in his life, at home and even in public. This doesn't mean they will be perfect all the time. Children are children and they will continue to do childish things, but what we say to them will always stay with them, whether good or bad. Today, we still speak good things into our children convinced that at some point in their lives they will recall words of life spoken to them. It's like depositing life saving words in them for when the right time comes those words will help and aid them. Another way I like to think about it is *sowing seed* into their lives. Somewhere in their life that seed will be watered, and will take root to a full bloom. What we say to our children now can also have an effect on where they're heading. The right words will help them learn to make better choices in life. A wise man once said,

"A lot of children have grown up to be more than what they thought they could be because someone else thought they could."

We have all experienced how a gentle word can turn away anger, fury, rage, and even bad temper (these, in some cases are referred to as *wrath.*) This specific nugget has become a favorite and a valuable tool for me, even to this day. Kind, gentle, sweet, loving, tender, good, affectionate, friendly and even helpful words can touch the heart of anyone, even a child in such a heavenly way that once applied, and the results taken to heart you will wish to talk that way all the time. This kind of transition or better defined as transformation takes time. *Why not start today!*

Now, to all of you who are married or ever hope to be this might be a golden nugget for you: *"One kind word can warm three winter months."* What a smart Japanese quote! Married or not, words can bring a warm feeling of security, love, and peace to us all. Try it, you'll like it.

Many of us have proven the fact that any gentle word works better than a non-gentle word. Sometimes it is tough to bite our tongue, not to mention how it hurts. The biting of the tongue here deals simply with *pride.* The verb "Pride" allows us to be proud of accomplishments, from our children, and our grandchildren, their cuteness, their intelligence and, most of all, of ourselves. This form of pride should encourage others. "Pride" as a noun, is where we have to be careful. Sometimes we tend to focus on *"me, myself and I"* type of pride. This form of *pride* is about self-esteem, self-respect, self-worth, self-importance, and self-love. Don't get me wrong, there should be proper respect for one's own dignity and worth, but be careful not to keep yourself to yourself. Your worth, your importance and your love should be shared with others for as long as you have breath. One way to share ourselves is by what we say. If we want to have a great family, we must learn to speak words of greatness over each member, including ourselves. If we are to have a great marriage, we must learn to speak life into it. Speaking to the marriage is literally speaking to your spouse. Of course there are times when we can't or choose not to speak kindly, so then we must not speak at all. Even my five year old grandson knew this quote by heart,

"If you can't say anything nice, don't say anything at all."

"Do you want a long, good life?" The book of Psalms asks the question and even gives us the answer, *"Then watch your tongue! Keep your lips from lying"* (Psalm34:12-13). Most of us would ask, *"Why would what I speak give me a longer life?"* Good question! This is the best way to put it; *"The words you speak are your life you live."*

Going back to my younger years, I recall my dad asking each one of his eleven children what we wanted for Christmas. Since we were only allowed one request, we spoke wisely. Afterwards Dad would say, *"You got it!"* Once our gift was opened on Christmas morning and if by chance one of us would have forgotten our spoken choice, Dad would remind us, *"You have what you said now do with it whatever you want."* This golden nugget not only taught me to be careful in what I asked for, but to be careful in what I spoke as well.

Conglomerated Heart

Have you ever seen a conglomerated rock or shell? I hadn't until recently while walking on the beach and squashing the sand between my toes, I came upon an unusual looking shell, hardly recognizable. Its round form was a mass made up of pebbles, sand, and even some smaller shells with tiny noticeable life forms within it cemented together in hard clay. Fascinated with this discovery, I became intrigued with the conglomerated shell. After thoroughly examining this cluster, I became aware that all through life one comes into all sorts of opportunities, some good, some not-so good, and still others not good at all. As the rock or the shell, we tumble here and there, and even get hurt a time or two, coming out with little bits of shells and pebbles still attached to our lives, and sometimes with little or no indication that our heart is being affected and formed in such a manner. What we have taken into our heart has become hard as clay, cemented and clustered together with confusion thus becoming as the conglomerated rock or shell.

Much the same happens because of the words spoken to us or by us. Whether we want to believe it or not, *words* from others have a strong affect on our lives, and what we say probably affects more people than any other action we take. One sure key to affecting others properly lies in who we are and how we speak. It is wise to give special attention to words and how they are used. We absorb all kinds of words on a daily basis through television, media, newspaper, and people such as parents, friends or teachers. This is where personal choice comes in. We all have the same choice whether to believe them, receive them or repeat them. If we assume control over any one of these choices, they instantly become a deposit in our heart and it is by these deposits that our mouth will speak. In other words, what we say reveals what is in our heart.

"For a man's heart determines his speech"
(Matthew 12:34 LV).

In nurturing eleven children, Mom and Dad had great control in regards to not allowing any cursing or fighting in the house. We seldom heard a "bad" word, but when we did, we instantly knew it was *bad*. It was obvious that the setting, the tone of voice and the reaction of the second party was a dead giveaway regarding it as a *bad* word! It wasn't until I became a teenager that I first heard a really bad word. At one time when my two older brothers were verbally fighting, out came a word I had never heard before. I knew it was *bad*, it sounded *bad*, and it even felt *bad* coming out of my brother's mouth. Giving attention to the new-found bad word I had just heard, I pondered on it for a moment. It was at this moment, as a bystander observing how the bad word was used, that it became a deposit in my own heart. Despite the fact that it had no meaning or significance to me didn't keep me from entertaining it in my mind. But then, a few weeks later I had gotten into a terrible verbal dispute with my sister, upsetting me to the bone. Before realizing what was coming out of my mouth, I heard that *bad* word slip out! Equally shocked with mouths open, we stared at each other for a frozen moment. Instantly, I knew I was in deep trouble and at a point of no return. Mother definitely dealt with me, which to this day I haven't forgotten. Unaware of the hidden bad word that was deposited in my heart, it conveniently slipped out at an uncontrollable moment. Whether it was my sister telling on me or her witnessing my adjustment, I'm sure she didn't allow it to be a deposit in *her* heart because in all the years I've known her, I've never heard her use any bad words. This was of course at the time when we didn't hear a lot of bad language. How much more do we have to be careful today with our children? Now, do you catch the significant of what it means to be careful what you hear and take into your heart? How about our children, what are they exposed to? What are their little hearts taking in?

In my younger years, I was aware that my heart was a very important organ, but yet not quite understanding its full significance to my life. Like most young girls, I thought the heart was the place for feelings I had for whomever, whenever, and forever. At that time it seemed crystal clear that my heartbeat was simply the evidence of being in love. It wasn't until much later in life that I encountered the true meaning of my heart and why I had to guard it.

"The heart is the wellspring of life."

It is a fact that our speech and actions reveal our real underlying beliefs. The good impressions we try to make cannot last if our hearts are deceptive. By now we understand that whatever is in the heart overflows into our speech. Isn't it interesting that an ancient family physician named Luke wrote, *"A good man out of the good treasure of his heart brings forth good; and an evil man out of the evil treasure of his heart brings forth evil.*

For out of the abundance of the heart his mouth speaks." We should all think of our heart as a treasure box, filled with the finest *word* treasures available to us.

"For where your treasure is, there will your heart be also" (Matthew 6:21 NKJ).

Our loyalty should be to the treasures of our heart. Be assured that heart treasures will never fade, cannot be stolen or used up, and will never wear out. We should teach our youngsters how to accumulate valuable treasure that can out last their lives.

Now, knowing that whatever is deposited in our heart will eventually come out of our mouth when the time of decision to speak becomes available, will we speak *words* of life or *words* of death? Good check point.

Ears are intake valves that feed our mind raw materials which can be converted into creative power. Hearing draws *words* into our mind. Choose wisely whether to believe and receive or ignore. Ignoring worthless *words* keeps our hearts from worthless deposits. We can quickly learn to reject *words* that are harmful. Learning to be careful in what we listen to, what we see, and even what we read is a lesson passed on to our own children. All sorts of *words*, ideas, sounds and sights penetrate our mind and heart and ultimately come out through our speech. The goal is to develop controlled speech patterns and habits that will contribute to our success, teaching us how to speak with authority. Just by cleaning up our speech we can solve a heart problem: *ours*!

Generally, we are mostly known by what we say and do. Unfortunately, it's obvious that to our children, our actions speak louder than our words. They are not only listening, but they are watching. How many parents are surprised when they witness their child for the first time repeating or acting out something inappropriate?

As a kindergarten teacher, I enjoyed the beautiful sight of children playing house, but it quickly saddened me seeing them become violent with the baby dolls. Another time, I watched as a little girl, role playing a part of mommy, washing dishes in the little play kitchen set up for playtime. Listening carefully, I could hear her talking to herself. I soon realized that she was arguing, saying she hated doing the dishes and she always had to clean up after everyone. Even in her roughing up the dishes made me realize that she must have seen that behavior along with the words she spoke somewhere in someone's home. We can't always help it if our children hear what they are not supposed to hear, but I learned a long time ago, good manners and respect cover a lot of ground when they are taught and practiced at home. Even adults can practice good manners and respect at home when we come to realize that we are a home of excellence.

Here is a really neat poem that fits this chapter and will give us something to think about:

Child-Proof

Holding a newborn in my arms,
I vow to protect from all harms.
Child-proofed my home from A to Z,
Removing dangers I could see.

With time the things from one so small,
Broke my heart from words and all.
So much I saw and heard that day,
Was it me? I'm ashamed to say.

Clearly knowing what I must do,
Child-proof myself and start anew.
This precious child in my arms,
I vow to protect from all harms.
-MAE

We are often judged by the words we speak, and how we use them. How do we want others to see us? Sometimes, unaware, our speech patterns are picked up by others including our very own children. Below are four common speech patterns that we all need to be aware of:

The Controlled Tongue:

When we have control of our tongue, we think before we speak, know when silence is best, and give wise advice.

"A good man thinks before he speaks"
(Proverbs 15:28 LV).

The Caring Tongue:

When we care for others we speak truthfully while seeking to encourage.

"A wise man speaks what is right and true and his advice is wholesome and good" (Proverbs 8:7 LV).

The Conniving Tongue:

A person with this type of speech is filled with wrong motives, gossip, slander, and twisted truth.

"...to slander is to be a fool" (Proverbs 10:18 LV).

The Careless Tongue:

This person's words are filled with lies and curses; he is quick-tempered, which can lead to rebellion and destruction.

"A fool's mouth is his destruction" (Proverbs 18:7 LV).

Now, where should we be fitting in?

The tongue, lips and mouth are closely associated with the heart. Yet a small thing, it can cause enormous damage! We cannot master self-control if we do not control what we say. If we can control this small, but powerful member, we can control the rest of our body.

Controlling Our Tongue Aides in Guarding Our Heart.

At times our thinking gets us into serious trouble. Negative thoughts such as fear, doubt or unbelief start working in our mind causing depression and weakness. Like it or not, when our mind ponders on negative thoughts we tend to speak them forth. To cast out negative thoughts from our mind, we must think positive, and meditate on good and healthy things which promote favorable speech. Another approach of getting away from the negative is to get around *good friends* that can encourage and lift us up. Their positive *words* will bring life to our situations, challenging us to grow. We should try to surround ourselves with only positive people. Their encouraging *words* will help break down the layers of our conglomerated heart.

Below is some wise advice given by a man named Paul in his book, *Ephesians*;

1. *"Don't use bad language, speak only what is good and helpful, and only what will bless"* (4:29).
2. *"Let no man deceive you with empty words"* (5:6).
3. *"Be careful how you live; these are difficult days"* (5:15).
4. *"Don't be fools, be wise; make the most of every opportunity for doing good"* (5:16).
5. *"Don't act thoughtlessly; find out what is right and do it"* (5:17).
6. *"Don't drink too much wine, for many evils lie along the path"* (5:18).
7. *"Give thanks always for all things"* (5:20).

Listening to the right words is as a well of life.

See No Evil, Hear No Evil, Speak No Evil And Do No Evil

The word "evil" is such a dark, eerie and mysterious word. This word definitely fits its sound. Generation after generation, people have quoted *"see no evil, hear no evil, and speak no evil."* Personally adding, *"do no evil"* to the quotation finalized its message to me. There's a lot of free beneficial advice in sayings such as these, but how many of us really take them serious?

Visualize four little monkeys sitting together, one with its eyes covered for; *see no evil, one's* ears covered for; *hear no evil,* the mouth covered for *speak no evil,* and, of course, the *do no evil* is left up to our own creative version of how else *evil* is believed to be done. Somehow the affect is not the same illustrated through a line of monkeys with their ears, eyes, and mouth covered up. Undoubtedly, you and I know it has nothing to do with monkeys. Although cleverly rendered, what kind of evil can a monkey do anyway? What we're about to learn isn't about monkey business, it's totally about people business. One way possible to keep from doing evil or wrong is by our talk.

In a nutshell, "evil" is morally bad or wrong. It is also wicked and sinful. In some cases, "Evil" with a capital "E" stands for that which is destructive or corruptive. Breaking down the definition into morsel size, impelled me to search the root word of "sinful." We're all familiar with the fact that *sin* is to do wrong. Some synonyms of *sinful* include bad, corrupt, wicked, and morally wrong. In my understanding, *moral* pertains to our personal behavior measured by principle standards of our intellectual judgment of right or wrong, which reflects our character. Since evil injures and is harmful, it is categorized as sin. In plain English, this virtually means that *evil,* in all probability, is wrong for mankind!

Expanding on the meaning of *sin*, I'll include a saying I've hear quite often: "Sin is *not doing* what you know is right." I wonder if it would hold true for, "Sin is *not saying* what you know is right." A lot of destructive and corruptive works are the results of things not being done or said at all. Don't get me wrong, this is not implying that *we* are evil or doing evil, it's just that I wonder how many different circumstances, events and lives could have been different if the *right things* had been done, or the *right words* had been spoken at their appointed time? It is hard to be bold all the time. At some point we've all been shy, afraid, or even embarrassed to speak up or do right, but if we knew without a doubt that our *right words* or our *right actions* would make a great difference in someone's life, wouldn't we want to do it? Of course we would. Mankind is always searching to do the right thing—it is our nature. Even growing up, facing obstacles in our lives, we often went to our parents for advice and direction because we wanted to make sure we were doing the right thing, right? *"Search your heart"* or *"Follow your heart"*, is still the best advice any parent or guardian can give their children. We were all designed to want to do the right thing. We just have to try to make the right choice.

"...Listen and understand it is not what goes into your mouth that makes you unclean, but it is what you say and think that makes you unclean" (Matthew 15:11 NIV).

In other versions of the above text, *makes you unclean,* is translated as *defiles you.* In addition, *defile* also means to corrupt the purity or perfection of something or someone, or to contaminate, and dishonor. Now, read the reference above with this new understanding. Wow! With this understanding we must not only want to guard our heart from what we see, hear, speak and do, but also by what we *think.* What comes out of your mouth can very well dishonor us.

Where does any child receive their first lessons? The answer is in the home where Mom and Dad are their first teachers. They learn about the use of *words*, and the authority they have. Even an infant quickly figures out that a word sounding like *Mom* catches someone's attention and causes change, and by this I don't mean only a diaper change. When he's hungry or tired, the word *Dad* works just as well. We are first-hand witnesses of their first lesson—*the power of words!* Even their little young minds understand the concept of their *words* in action. This is their first step in speaking. Think about it, with every new word they learn and say, we get all crazy and silly. All this time thinking they knew the meaning of what they were saying. No! They just experienced the power behind their words. Most young infants mimic their parent's speech and behavior much through most of their life living under the same roof. Parents are as a motion picture before their children's eyes. As will be mentioned later, all movies have specific ratings for specific age groups. So my question is, what rating would you put on your speech and behavior when you're around your children? Good check point.

Parents must be well-advised as to whom they entrust their children when they are seeking childcare or education. Don't let others convince you of direction for your children's lives unless you totally trust them and you yourself have checked out such avenues or sources. Only then will you be assured that what your children see and hear will be safe for them, and will not contradict with your own views, values, and principles at home. Whatever your life status is pertaining to your children, it is important to start them early by filling their hearts with fine treasures beginning with a decent vocabulary in your selected language. Equip them early.

Any language consists of a specific vocabulary, which is the variety of the speaker's stock of words or of their source. Our language applies primarily to verbal expression with reference to the words or vocabulary used. Speech, our spoken language, may draw attention to excellence or inappropriate use of our words, to their dignity or their indecency, to their fitness or lack of fitness, or to any of the qualities which speech may derive from the choices we make in life. We have all heard that there is style in how one speaks. This manner of expressing one's thoughts or emotions through speech very well characterizes the speaker. How do we, as parents, want to be characterized by our children's friends or their teachers? How about our friends, our leaders, our mentors, our students, our spouses, our relatives, and our peers, what category do they see us in?

In an earlier chapter, I mentioned how the *words* we speak reveal our heart. Many times, our words paint a picture of ourselves to others. The following quote from Ben Jonson seems to back up this truth.

"Language must show a man; speak, that I may see you."

Did you know that *Gone with the Wind* was the first family movie to use a profane word? I'm sure the reaction must have been startling to many viewers. Even hearing it for the first time caused my ears to perk up and left me somewhat speechless. We the people justified the case, thinking, what harm can one little word do? This kind of compromising was what brought change to the family film industry. Unfortunately, with each year there are new words added and accepted or tolerated by the people. Unaware, that in tolerating the use of such profane language, by definition we permitted it. We even recognized and respected rights, opinions or practices of others, whether agreeing with them or not. Sometimes it's easier to tolerate such films, and in doing so, we find ourselves putting up and bearing them, but worse of all we just endure them. Now we have a whole list of words thrust at us and our children from supposedly non-violent family films. Remember our children are little magnets, they pick up everything.

There's this thing called "ratings" for movies and television, even though we don't understand all the conformations of it, it's not a surprise that the Motion Picture Association of America (MPAA) and the Television Content Rating Systems are continually and equally attacked by free-speech activists and conservative critics concerning their standards of rating. According to the MPAA review, a Harvard study suggested that in 2003, more *inappropriate* content had been allowed in PG and PG-13 rated movies than ten years prior. Wow, it's no wonder that with this type of information anyone can ask, "What's the use in trying to change anything?" The study suggests that whatever the case, the Decent Films rule of thumb continues to apply—parents shouldn't count on the MPAA rating system to do their job for them. No matter what the rating, *parental guidance* is always required. Absolutely a plus! We can start at home! In our own home we had a personalized rating system—MPAAH (Motion Picture Association of the Archila Home.) This may be silly to some, but not everything on television or in movies was allowed to be viewed by our family. We might not have control in the American home, but we do have absolute control in our own homes in the care and upbringing of one or more valuable future leaders. Actually, they are our *only* hope for solving tomorrow's problems.

Once a child knows what he or she is allowed to watch, they can take great pride in knowing they, too, can make wise choices especially if you commend them for it. My grandchildren are prime examples of this. At the time when my grandson was just a toddler, if there was any program or commercial on TV that he knew he wasn't allowed to watch he would instantly cover his eyes and say so. The older he got, he still announced his boundaries, and switched the channels all by himself. Today, he and his younger sister are aware of the ratings on movies, music, games and even toys. I have even witnessed him saying that he had to walk away from certain kids because they were talking improper. Even in my car they'll inform me that a certain song, because of the lyrics, is not safe for their ears. The only credit I take in having good grandchildren is that I had a good daughter that became a good mother. Remember, it starts at home.

When parents teach a child how to make decisions, they don't have to watch them every step of the way. We must give them room to exercise their ability to make choices and right decisions for themselves, whether easy or difficult, whether right or wrong. Just letting them know we are always there for them will give them confidence.

"Train a child in the way he should go,
and when he is old he will
not turn from it"
(Proverbs 22:6 NIV).

You've heard the saying: *"Start where you're at."* Better yet, to make it more personal; *"Start with what you have in your hand."* What you have in your hand is a book of golden nuggets that you can read over and over to help keep you focused on knowing that you do have a valuable part in life for yourself and your love ones. If you make a difference to only one person, you have changed something in that person's life, even if that person is *you.*

CHAPTER TWO

Seeds

Sowing

This chapter is about sowing *seeds*, not the kind you sow in the ground, but the kind that are sown in you. Many of the illustrations will be in reference to the natural seed. For most of us, there are lessons after lessons in nature itself. There's certainly a lot to learn from just looking around, listening, and simply paying attention to the beauty of nature.

First of all, we all know that a "seed" is that which is capable of producing into an individual similar to that from which it derives its origin. When we sow seed, we are scattering, planting or seeding with purpose in mind. I personally like the word *seedsman*, which is a person who deals in seeds or one who scatters seed. Every person has seeds to sow. In addition to our words, we can also sow our time and talent into others.

How many people in our life time, have been affected by the seed we have scattered, through merely the words we've spoken? It's possible that the million or more words that have come out of our mouths have gone out as seeds even before we were able to understand this principle. If we could see our words floating around, what would they look like, better yet, what would they be doing?

Growing up in the country, I became familiar with the planting of a garden. With a handful of seeds, I was instructed to drop one in each hole dug in the freshly prepared soil. The seed was then covered up with the precise amount of soil neither being too deep nor too shallow. It was then watered and cared for in the coming weeks until it became what it was suppose to become according to what kind of seed was planted. This went on throughout the entire garden, sowing and planting different seeds all which had their soil prepared accordingly. Once the roots took and the plant appeared, the real work began. Our job was to help the plant survive according to what it was meant to be. The picking of weeds, plucking dried leaves, pruning and watering helped the plant grow healthier and stronger. Lots of care was necessary to reap a good crop, right? Our words to our children work the same way. Think about our children as our little gardens, needing our care until full grown.

In relating this concept to words here's a cute, but meaningful lesson for us who scatter seed with care:

1. Choose your seeds (*words*) properly.
2. Prepare your seeds (*words*) in proper soil.
3. Sow your seeds (*words*) in correct manner.
4. Care for your seed (*word*) so it will produce a good crop.
5. Enjoy your seed (*word*) as it produces fruit.

We've all heard these sayings; *"What you sow, you will reap."* What about this saying; *"What goes around, comes around."* Words work in the same manner. If they are good words they will produce good works, but if they are bad words they will produce bad works. Many times we have sown the wrong seeds (words), at the wrong time, in the wrong place, therefore our harvest becomes questionable. Our children become confused as well, when wrong seeds (words) are sown in them. Sometimes we will have to pluck or prune our little plants depending on the seeds we have sown. Just remember to work your garden with care.

Many times I hear "The Golden Rule" misquoted as; *"Do unto others as they do unto you."* This is what the book of wisdom says, *"Do not say, I'll do to him as he has done to me"* (Proverbs 24:29 NIV). The correct quote is as follows:

"Do unto others as you would have them do unto you."

"As you would have them do unto you" requires you sowing good seed into their lives, so you will receive a good return by them sowing good seed into your life. This changes the meaning totally. The two sayings are opposite of each other; the first one is *attacking* the second one is *protecting.* We must protect our seed being careful where we sow it. Look for good ground. Your children are good ground, they are *you* extended into the future. Sowing into their lives is an investment.

Remember children are little sponges, they absorb, and many times without question or reason. It is a wonderful feeling to see your children behaving in the manner that you taught them from youth, but it's a better feeling to hear that they are behaving when you are not around. This is the strong foundation all parents want for their children. When my grandchildren were smaller they often surprised me with their affirm remarks towards a particular subject. For instance, I would ask them if they wanted some ice cream. They would answer, *"Yes, but I have to ask my mom if I'm allowed to have it."* It was the same thing was with candy, movies, toys, etc. They knew what was acceptable and allowed, even away from home. My daughter and her husband spoke into their children's lives according to how they should be brought up. Their goal is for their children to become decent, respectable, honest, intelligent, and responsible adults. Their focus is on the *adult* their child is to become. Therefore, they are not only raising children, they are raising adults. Their words have been chosen to bring a future life to their children.

One lesson all parents, guardians, teachers and other caregivers of children should take into consideration as a golden nugget is to never "label" a child, especially when we're angry with them for doing something wrong. We often hear parents shouting to their children in public places such words as, *"You are so stupid!"* or *"How much dumber can you get?"* Then we wonder why children have problems believing in themselves and later kicking themselves saying, *"I can't believe I'm so stupid!"* I've often wondered how Charlie Brown felt when he kept being called "stupid" by his friend in the kid's movie, *Merry Christmas, Charlie Brown.*

One way to avoid *labeling* a child, when they're misbehaving, is by simply asking them why they are behaving, acting, or pretending as such. Then you back it up with saying they are not in any manner what they are behaving, acting or pretending to be. My favorite example to my children when they were caught jumping on the bed or the couch, was; *"Why are you behaving like monkeys? I don't remember bringing any monkeys home from the hospital."* This approach always brought the laughter, but they would stop the jumping without feeling labeled. This works with other such words as, stupid, dumb, crazy and so forth. Parents, do whatever works best, they are your children. Your words should be good, life-filled words. Knowing what right words to speak helps you to do the right thing around your children.

Our former President, Lyndon B. Johnson quoted in his 1965 speech:

"A President's hardest task is not to do what is right, but to know what is right."

Even a simple smile can be returned immediately upon one occurrence. What about a wave or a hello? There are very friendly states where one can travel through and get free smiles, hellos, and waves to every mile. One summer driving through Texas, a person waved at me casually as we passed each other on the highway. My first reaction was to wave back, later asking myself, *"Who was that?"* There are just plain nice folks sowing nice seeds. We might never know these folks, nor ever see them again, but that seed will still produce after its kind. The truth is *a smile is contagious,* for that matter, so is a wave and a hello. Sometimes we forget that the finest things within us can be sown in others as seeds. Sometimes, it just might be the right time to smile or wave to someone.

As a kindergarten teacher, I gave away a lot of smiles. The children knew a little game I played and they got a thrill out of it every time. Each time a child entered into the class with a frown

I'd ask, *"Where is your smile, did you leave it at home?"* Offering them *mine,* and pretending to put it upon their little face, instantly produced a smile. All day long they would wear *my* smile proudly. Many great seeds are sown in the lives of small children, but a hug and a smile returned touch the very soul. Many teachers today are experiencing a perpetual harvest of hugs and smiles from an adult, at one time being that little child in their arms.

Another thing to be careful of is not to "compare" children to other children especially to siblings. *"Why can't you be like your brother?"* Such words as these can quench their little dreams, *"Oh, look how pretty she is, I wish you'd grow up to be just like her."* If a child is or looks nothing like what she is compared to, she will soon come to realize that she has failed her parents and herself. Some things that are said to a child can stay with them for a long time. Choosing the right words can be a bridge to a child's future, and building them up means building stronger bridges for them.

Being the oldest girl of eleven children, gave me a perfect stage to play and pretend to be *the teacher.* I would spend lots of precious hours tracing and retracing pages after pages for all my little students. A school house of king-size sheets overlaying chairs, stools and boxes, was always an amazing classroom set up with pillows as chairs for my younger siblings, which often complimented me saying, *"You're such a good teacher."* Even at age ten, words influenced me in desiring to become a great teacher. Teachers are significant to our future. What an honor! As Henry Adams quoted:

"A teacher affects eternity; he can never tell where his influence stops."

The motto for Kean College, New Jersey, quoted by John Cotton Dana reads, *"Who dares to teach must never cease to learn."* We have a whole world ahead of us to teach through our children. Why not start now? Are you ready? Start sowing!

The Heart of the Matter

Earlier, we learned that the "heart" is the vital center of one's being, emotions, and sensibilities. Many know it to be the seat of emotions, inner strength or character, and the central or innermost part of us. The heart is our life. We need to learn how to care for it. Just as our physical heart is the supplier of the blood to the rest of our physical body; likewise, our minds and our mouths are the treasure suppliers to our heart. This can't be seen with the natural eye, but as blood runs through our veins to give us life, so does the treasures within our heart.

"It is only with the heart that one can see rightly; what is essential is invisible to the eye."
–ANTOINE DE SAINT-EXUPERY

"Wherever your treasure is, there your heart and thoughts will also be." In Luke 12:24, it clearly states that whatever condition our treasure is in, it will reflect our heart and thoughts; therefore revealing our true priorities. We cannot separate our actions from our beliefs. Just as we need to check ourselves before acting out, same goes for checking our words before speaking to accurately reflect treasure values?

As a reminder, deposits of the heart come by what we see, hear and read. We've heard the expression, *"...wearing one's heart on one's sleeve."* This means to show ones' feelings clearly by ones' behavior. Sometimes we don't even have to talk to show what's in our heart. At times our actions are louder than words. As we all know, children learn values and morals, and priorities by observing how their parents act and react every day. Again, be careful what goes into your heart, sooner or later it will be revealed.

"Children have never been very good at listening to their elders, but they have never failed to imitate them."
-JAMES BALWIN

The above quote holds true even for those who don't have children or may rarely be around them. Just as we watch people, people watch us. Our children, (the people of the future) are tapping into our doings. Some may want to imitate us or some may just not like us at all, either way, they are watching. Whether we care, or not, we are still influencing someone, and no one is exempt from what comes out of their own heart. Your heart is the invisible *you*, because out of the abundance of it, your mouth will speak. Another translation for abundance is *overflow*. Wouldn't it be nice to have our hearts overflowing with good treasure? How about our children's hearts?

Now, let's examine Matthew 15:18; *"But those things which proceed out of the mouth come forth from the heart."* Here *proceed* means to come out or once begun, it continues. Sometimes when we get into a rage or even an uncontrollable moment or situation, our mouth starts up and sometimes it continues and continues. At times we will discover things in our heart that aren't right, but remember we all have the power to control our tongues from speaking inappropriate things or keep from hurting others as well as ourselves. We've all heard this before, *"If I listen to you long enough, I can tell what kind of person you are."* This can be pretty scary, but one way to make sure that what others are hearing through us is coming from a pure heart revealing who we really are. It is wise to always be on top of your treasure by simply guarding your heart. Guarding our heart means guarding our treasure. Guarding it from what goes in and what comes out.

"Guard your heart, for out of it are the issues of life" (Proverbs 4:23 KJV).

In chapter one, we defined *life* as the present state of existence or energy. Now, as we read the above quote it can very well mean that out of our hearts flow whatever pertains to our present state of existence and our energy! This is definitely something to think about! Would our heart reveal the good results of our life?

Building our heart's treasure according to the kind of man or woman we want to be, requires the finest of the finest deposits we can possess. Treasures not only come by what we hear and see, they also come by what we think and say about ourselves. Ask yourself, will the treasures in your heart reveal to your children the true you? In the same manner our children's treasures should also reveal themselves, not just at home, but wherever they go.

"For as a man thinks in his heart, so is he"
(Proverbs 23:7 KJV).

Publilius Syrus once wrote; *"No man is happy who does not think himself so."* Wouldn't it be something else, if we just thought on good, pure, happy and great things? How different would we be if we thought ourselves happy or successful, or even prosperous? What would our heart say about our thinking? As a young girl at home, I'd often go to my mom or dad for advice on whether I should do this or that. My dad, the wise man that he is, would ask me, *"Well, what do you think you should do?"* He would conclude with this; *"Don't listen to your head, listen to your heart."* This kind of wisdom surrounds us daily, and much of it has been around since our childhood. It's time to have an ear to hear and a mind to understand. If you need a good challenge, surround yourself with wisdom and see what happens.

One evening I was watching a documentary on television about *lions* in South Africa. In certain flooded areas these lions have adapted for survival purposes. What we believed to be true about cats hating water definitely didn't apply with these giant cats. These lions had adapted to hunting in the waters and even their coats had thickened to withstand the cold water at night. Many of us have adapted to our surroundings. Some adaptation for us is not always the best choice to go. This kind of harmful change is seen more in children than in adults. If a child is suddenly surrounded by lifestyles or habits different than he's used to, he tends to adapt to fit in. The change becomes easier the longer he's surrounded by such. His vocabulary changes, his style of fashion, his hair style and even his walk. Those around him begin to take notice, especially his parents. The more he follows, the more he imitates. In some extreme cases, it becomes very difficult to change them and God forbid they get into trouble of some sort. It's never too late to be there for them. Children often test life, seeking acceptance wherever they might think they fit in, therefore tolerating the environment that surrounds them.

"It is easy to be tolerant when you do not care."
–CLEMENT F. ROGERS

If we don't care about our children, then they won't care about themselves. Then for sure we would all be in the same boat as Alice in *Alice's Adventures in Wonderland* by Lewis Carroll;

"Would you tell me, please which way I ought to go from here?"
"That depends a good deal on where you want to go to." said the cat.
"I don't much care where-," said Alice.
"Then it doesn't matter which way you go." said the cat.

Being like Alice, means that we don't care which way we go or which way we're going. It is important that we care and that our children know that we care. We need to care for their present as well as their future. Let them know it by being there for them and talking to them about what *they* want to talk about. At times we must only listen, and show them respect and love on a daily basis. Tell your children they are going into a great future and see what they say.

No one said parenting was going to be easy, but if the challenge is worth the future, why not give it our best. At times, children might not seem to listen to us, but they *are,* and our words are becoming deposits in them without them knowing. In my own household, raising teenagers wasn't a piece of cake. At times, when confronting them on particular problems they would give us the silent treatment. Though aggravated at their uncommunicativeness, it made it a perfect moment to deposit good, life-filled words into their hearts. At tender moments as these we must be careful to say what we mean, and even more so to mean what we say. Given the situation, it may seem as though they are not listening, but keep pouring your heart out to them. At some point, those same seeds will get watered and they will produce. We should *never* give up on our children or a child we care about. I truly believe they are gifts to us. This reminds me of a big bright yellow button I saw on the shoulder of a teacher, it read: *"Children are our gift from God, what we do with them is our gift to God."*

"No act of kindness, no matter how small,
is ever wasted."-AESOP, FABLES

We need to believe that we are capable of influencing many children and adults alike. Personally, I know my existence here isn't just for me alone. At some point in life almost everyone has wondered, *"Why am I here, anyway?"* As a favorite lesson to teach, I always found it interesting how others, especially children responded to my answer: *"We live our life for others."* Children found it funny when I would challenge them to hug themselves. Then I would ask them, *"Does it make you feel warm and fuzzy?"* Hugs are meant to give away. Life is not about *"give me, give it only to me, me, me, me."* It's not so much what others can do for us, but what we can do for others. Yes, our limbs and other parts of our bodies serve us well, but they can serve others better. Again, it's because we now understand that everything we do is sowing seed into others' lives. At this very moment whatever we have can be a tool or a vehicle to touch someone else, whether close to home or far away. It's not about us as *one,* it's about us as *one in unity*, working together to make a better world.

"Down in the hearts, wise men know the truth: the only way to help yourself is to help others."
-ELBERT HUBBARD

We can hear and read about *wisdom* and *knowledge* and even see its effects all around us in different forms and shapes. It's all free for the taking, to experience it for ourselves.

"Nothing ever becomes real 'til it is experienced - even a proverb is no proverb to you 'til your life has illustrated it."
-JOHN KEATS, LETTER (1819)

Believe it or not, there is a difference between *wisdom* and *knowledge.* "Wisdom" is an understanding of what is true, right, or lasting. Having wisdom or better yet, being wise means you are sensible, you have common sense, good judgment, and discernment for the right things. A wise man is known for having great learning; and is highly educated. Wisdom involves the ability to apply what has been acquired mentally to the conduct of one's affairs.

"Knowledge," on the other hand, is fact of knowing something with familiarity, awareness, or understanding gained through experience or study. If you are knowledgeable it is proper to say that you are well-informed.

Have you ever heard that good teaching comes from good learning? We should value our good teachings through the years. Many good teachers have sown into my life, as I'm sure in yours as well. No matter how many more years I have to live, I hope to acquire a lot more good learning. There are no better alternatives to learning wisdom, we are either becoming wise learners or refusing to learn and becoming foolish failures. As parents and teachers we will come across that one or two or maybe even more persons who don't have any desire to learn. In most cases, these are older children or adults, which make it hard to change. Now, in a young child, we still respect their level of understanding depending on maturity. As they develop their understanding, we can further their teaching. The younger the child, the easier the teaching, but in any case, no one should ever give up on any child or adult for that matter. Our job is to prepare our children and present them to the future one day at a time. As far as adults go, we can also start sowing seeds into their lives, speaking wisely around them and to them.

How the *wise* learns versus why the *fool* fails:

1. The *wise* gladly receives instruction and criticism, while the *fool* ignores instruction all together.
2. The *wise* accepts discipline and chooses who to listen to, while the *fool* doesn't learn from his mistakes.
3. The *wise* profits from constructive criticism, while the *fool* self-destructs by refusing criticism.
4. The *wise* desires to be taught, listens to others, and asks for advice, but the *fool* refuses reproof, thinks he needs no advice, and plunges ahead.

We've all been there and know how hard it is to learn from a mistake we didn't acknowledge making. What good is a mistake if we don't learn from it? To learn from an error we need to admit it, analyze it, and make adjustments so that we don't make the same mistake twice. Everyone makes mistakes, but let's not continue to be foolish and repeat them.

Something in each one of us strongly resists admitting we are wrong. That is why we admire people who openly and graciously admit their mistakes. These people have a strong self-image. They do not always have to be right to feel good about themselves. We, as well, must be willing to reconsider—to admit we are wrong, and to change our plans when it is necessary. These are the things our children are seeing in us. As adults, we are not immune to making mistakes, but if we're wise about handling our mistakes in life, our children will benefit from the lesson.

You can't have wisdom without knowledge, but you can have knowledge without wisdom. Head knowledge can get you nowhere if you think you know it all. The world is full of people who work hard to make others think they are smart. The books they carry, the facts they quote, or even the friends they hang out with are impressive. These foolish individuals don't want to be instructed, and they think it shows weakness to learn from others. They are wrong! Listening to others is a sign of wisdom, not weakness, but refusing to learn from others can be a great mistake. This can cause a person who could have been successful, to fail. In all certainty, tapping into the resources of wisdom will change your life from smart to wise. A wise person is a model of a meaningful life. His sense of purpose attracts others who want to know how they too can find meaning. This opens up a field of opportunities to sow seed. We would all desire to be wise, not wise guys, but wise for the sake of our well being.

Since ancient times, wisdom has served teachers, parents, and guardians. Today, by following the pointers listed below, when dealing and raising our children, we can be assured that seeds of wisdom can also take root in their lives by our example.

- Given advice should be refreshing and encouraging, (Read Proverbs 13:14).
- Make learning a joy for your learners, (Read Proverbs 15:2; 16:21).

- Give wise advice—right words at the right time, (Read Prov. 15:23; 18:20).

If wisdom could talk, it would say, *"Pay attention and listen to the sayings of the wise; apply your heart to what I (wisdom) teach, for it is pleasing when you keep them in your heart and have all of them ready on your lips."* There are a lot of benefits designated for the wise. If earning an authentic reputation for wisdom interests you, read the entire Book of Proverbs.

It's not what you know, but what you do with what you know that counts.

Word's Echo

"Echo" is a repetition or imitation of something, as the opinions, speech, or dress of another. It's funny to think that we are all echoing our life.

"In fact, nothing is said that has not been said before." –TERENCE

Have you ever heard your mom's words suddenly echoing out of your mouth, and catching yourself saying, *"Oh, my goodness, I sound just like my mom?"* Well, I have, and many more times than I can count. Even growing up, and well into my adult life, I still heard words echoing in my heart of what was said to me as a child. Children are a *catch-all* for words spoken around them. Though we might think that words or habits that echo from our past are passed down to us like hand-me-downs, they were only *seeds.* Our minds pick up on what we hear or see, causing them to become deposits in our hearts.

Not all words that echo in our lives are significant, neither are the things we do *just because.* In our past, we have done and said many things that are still done and said today without reason. Then there comes a moment in our life when we ask ourselves, *"Why do we do what we do or say what we say?"* Questioning moments like these, help us define significance in our lives. Once understanding whether such echoes or seeds are of value or not, we are instantly opened to change. Remember, change is good and it is required in order to move forward in life. Many of us have come across things in our lives that needed to change, whether it was in our speech, our way of dressing, our way of cleaning, cooking, talking to others or just in our way of thinking. We cannot stay in the past by not allowing ourselves, or our children to change. Being unique and different requires different changes in each one of us, as well as in our children. We are *not* clones, copies or duplicates of one another, therefore as we instill in our children values and principles, we are building *their* foundation for *their* life, not ours. Even though they'll start out their life with echoes, which most times are stepping stones, they will gradually think for themselves, do for themselves, all the while becoming their own selves. As they mature, insignificant words and actions will exit their life, but their foundation will remain. It's clear that we will see ourselves in our children. Our traits, features, and attributes are passed down through the genes, not the heart. These are gifts or seeds for them to become what they are supposed to become. Your good words, also gifts and seeds, will echo in their lives and fill their heart's treasure.

One precious memory comes to my mind pertaining to the echo of priceless seeds in my grandson and granddaughter's hearts. When my daughter graduated from college the children were five and two years old. We had reservations for a large party at a restaurant to celebrate our daughter's enormous accomplishment. After all food orders had been taken, we all waited patiently as each ones' plate arrived. Once the last plate was placed on the table, my grandson, a kindergarten graduate, proudly announced, *"I want to bless the food."* Together the two children held hands and reached out to the person on their right and left. With heads bowed, two little voices started to sing a *"Thank you God for the food"* song. This went on for a short time, but it was sufficient time to notice quietness that had overtaken the restaurant as the two small children led a whole party in prayer with a song. As soon as the last *"Amen"* was sung, opening our eyes and lifting our heads, we were touched by what we saw. The entire restaurant was standing around applauding the two small children that had a song in their hearts that echoed throughout the place.

What a treasure we all witnessed. This is why I can unquestionably agree that no matter how many persons rise up to remove prayer from our schools; they can't touch what is in our hearts. On the other hand, be aware that all kinds of words can be echoes in our lives; words can be good seeds that are vital to our future or words can be seeds that can destroy dreams of the future. Be wise—choose your words wisely. This poem paints a picture of how our own words go forth with purpose:

ECHOES

Scores of echoes heard faraway,
Mimicking life from a busy day;
Some lingering or lacking destiny,
Resting in the hearts of so many.

Many wrong words spoken out,
Done in whisper or in shout;
Suddenly pierces the finest heart,
Entrusted to us from the start.

Soon friends will become few,
If what our speaking lacks value.
A broken heart of a dear friend,
Needs no less than one word to mend.

If words were deeds of kindness,
Their echoes would mimic no less.
Just know there's power in your words,
To heal and strengthen family cords.

Before speaking, see what's near,
A mountain, a love one, they both can hear.
If not now, surely it won't be long,
You'll hear an echo whether right or wrong.
-MAE

In spite of being the oldest daughter, and learning from my mother and father all kinds of words, traits, habits, manners, qualities and characteristics, I still asked, *"Why?"* Needing to know why things were done or said a certain way was something I desired. That was the beginning of my learning about words. Our first son turned out just the same. Every time I would explain an issue to him, or make a comment on a particular subject he'd ask, *"Why?"* Think about this. If your child asks *why* to any one of your comments, would you be willing to answer him with a long boring speech? First of all, you would lose any child's interest in their waiting for an answer to their *why*, and second, if it's beyond their understanding, re-adjust your words to them. When children ask *why,* make your answers short, simple and valuable. What excites a young child, is not our intelligence, it's their understanding. I gauge my answers to children according to their age. A five year old has a solid attention span of five minutes. Those first five minutes are golden. The next five minutes are silver. This gauge can be applied to everyone. Did you ever notice, the older the person, the more golden moments you get? Why not find a wise person, full of years, and allow them to impart wisdom into your life.

"Youth is the age to receive instruction, middle age to make use of it, and old age to impart it to others."
–PYTHAGORAS

Curse Words

"Curse" is the evil or injury thus invoked by someone. It is also known to be that which brings or causes evil. Earlier, we learned that evil words destroy. You might ask, *"Destroy what?"* Well, let's see, words can be used either as weapons or tools, hurting relationships or building them up. Sadly, it is often easier to destroy than to build, and a lot of people have experienced more destructive words than words which build up. Words either demolish or construct. In fact, not all bad words are curse words, but just the same, they do some kind of damage. Some lives have really been messed up because of the curse words directed to them. Unfortunately, some of those lives are children.

Being married to an architect, has allowed me opportunities to see construction sites as well as demolition sites. At a construction site, even though there's building material and debris everywhere, something is being constructed. As time allows, the building starts to take form. Even with all the overtime work, the good and the bad weather, help or no help, the job still gets done. Within a short time, the new building is finished. On the other hand, the demolition site also has debris everywhere, which seems to pile up more and more every day. Even if a problem arises, in tearing down a wall, a roof, the foundation, etc…, without a doubt, it still has to come down. There have been many buildings and houses, which seemed to be in perfect condition that had to be demolished. For whatever reasons, maybe some just needed to be replaced by better and bigger buildings. The same may apply to us at times when we might need to make changes in our lives, or in the lives of others, like our children. We have to be careful not to demolish a life when it just needs a little remodeling. All Architects and Engineers step back and review the plans in order to know what needs to be done before starting, likewise, we have to make sure that we are constructing and building a life and not destroying it, because remember, at the beginning it all starts out the same way. It can get pretty messy, not to mention difficult, as we get rid of the stuff that is not important and replace it with valuable treasure. Our words *will* make a difference. Only you can choose them to be tools for destruction or tools for construction.

"Thou are snared with the words of thou mouth, thou art taken with the words of thy mouth."
(Proverbs 6:2 KJV).

The word "snared" means to be trapped or entangled. Yes, our tongues can get us into a lot of trouble! Needless to say, *our* tongue is *our* responsibility, and only *we* can do something about it. Controlling our tongue from speaking out what is not right will keep us from being trapped or entangled by our own words. Our tongue is like a weapon, which is safe to say, it *can* do a lot of harm—not just to others; but to our own selves, as well. It was Washington Irving who said, *"A sharp tongue is the only edge tool that grows keener with constant use."* James said, *"The tongue is a fire...a restless evil and full of deadly poison."* and, *"The tongue is a small thing, but what enormous damage it can do"* (James 3:5 KJV).

But ah, we all agree, our tongue is helpful, it enables us to eat, taste and swallow and equally significant, it is the major organ of communication. Yet, how can one see it as the brutal beast it is, nicely tucked and hidden within the gates of our teeth? It can innocently curl itself up into a whistle, it can yawn, it can switch a piece of candy or gum from side to side to help us enjoy the flavor, and it even moistens our dried lips. But then, it can transform into its flip side of nature in an instance when it is bitten or when your thumb is smashed or even a toe jammed! It's at this point, when it is unthinkable to control your speech, but not impossible! This so call beast is untamable! *Taming* our tongue means we would have to overcome its wildness or make it less intense. Sadly speaking, we can't tame our tongue. The good news is that we *can* control it! Controlling our tongue means we can regulate it by exercising our authority over it to direct, to command, to restrain and to hold back from speaking what we should not speak. Each one of us has total authority over our own tongue. Our authority comes by mastering self-control, which not only helps us control what we say, but also what we *do*. If you can control this small but powerful member, you can control the rest of your body.

"Mend your speech a little, lest it may mar your fortunes."
- WILLIAM SHAKESPEARE

If we want to control our speech, we must:

- Speak right words
- Think before we speak
- Speak reasonable words
- Speak the truth

In teaching our children we need to understand how vital it is to *speak the right words.* Mark twain says, *"The difference between the almost right word and the right word is really a large matter–'tis the difference between the lightning-bug and the lightning."* Speaking the right words can be the bridge to success or the bridge to failure for yourself, your kids, your students, your co-workers, your family, or your friends. Take authority over your tongue, and speak the right words at the right time. A man named Heinrich Heine once said, *"God has given us tongues so that we may say something pleasant to our fellow man."*

Stopping to *think before speaking* is something everyone should practice. A wise person thinks before he speaks, because he wants to say what he knows in the best possible way. The foolish person doesn't wait to speak because he doesn't care about the affects of his words on others. It is important to have something to say, but it is equally important to say it well. Parents and teachers should always be searching for nuggets (words) of gold in educating children. Many times parents have had to count to ten, or so, before disciplining their child. *"Go to your room, I'll be there later!"* worked best for me. This allowed me sufficient time to cool off and think before speaking out. Even when a spanking is in order, it should be addressed and communicated to the child, as well as allowing them to communicate back, not talk back; there is a difference. Always allow your children to express themselves, especially if they are in trouble. This way they will learn the difference in communicating rather than talking back, especially to teachers and their elders. Around children, we need not let anger control our speech or actions. Humans often offend by words, whether in anger or not. So, think before the words come out!

"Delay is the best remedy for anger."-SENECA

Oliver Wendell Holmes puts it this way, *"Talking is one of the fine arts...and its fluent harmonies may be spoiled by the intrusion of a single harsh note."* In addition, Publilius Syrus wrote: *"He who conquers his wrath overcomes his greatest enemy."* I personally think it seems easier for most men to think before they speak. Could it be to the fact that most men (compared to most women) are known to be of little or fewer words? I see this in my husband, my sons and my son-in-law. These kind of men are known to be wise, have good sense, are trustworthy, have self control, have a settled mind, have careful speech, think before they speak, and stay out of trouble. Hurray for all our men who fall into this category!

"A bird is known by its note and a man by his talk."

My father often said, *"Whatever is worth doing at all is worth doing well."* Even though I didn't realize it then, he was quoting Lord Chesterfield. In adaptation to this book, I added my version, "*Whatever is worth saying at all, is worth saying well.*" As mentioned before, this kind of advice has been around forever, and I'm sure quotes have been quoted and re-quoted and so forth. When you hear; *"There's nothing new under the sun."* don't you think it applies to words as well?

The written word has so much potential for those who read it, but far more powerful for those who apply it. Wise words have been flowing around in hopes that the true basic foundations of human survival can credit them in some form. There's a truth to the following short poem I wrote called, *Wisdom*. As you read it, think about what we might be missing in not applying wisdom to our lives, especially in the way we speak.

WISDOM

Wisdom flows in quotes of old,
Free to all that take a hold.

Wisdom rules in hearts of men,
As lasting love there is no end.

Wisdom speaks of nothing new,
Yet changes hearts of more than few.

Wisdom lives forever now,
Free for all that know not how.
-MAE

I believe that even though we might not always understand how wisdom works, it works because it comes from the mind of God to the mind of man.

It is important to know how to *speak reasonable words.* We have an unlimited selection of words we use daily. In fact, it's not the quantity, but the quality of the words that you speak that will give you a good return. In previous chapters you read of words being seeds that bring forth life. The truth being that most reasonable words birth life into a situation, whether in correcting, instructing, or even in casual conversation. Reasonable words should be fair, rational, and governed by reason.

Once in a store, I heard a mother ordering her child not to dare touch whatever the child was reaching for. The child asked why she couldn't touch it. The mom's response was, *"Because I said so, that's why!"* The reason behind her answer has nothing to do with why the child cannot touch whatever she wasn't allowed to touch in the first place. Communication is not always the easiest route to take when you're in a hurry or the kids are acting up, but it is by far the best. No matter how many *whys* we hear in a day from our children, we should always try to give *reasonable* answers.

"Politeness cost nothing and gains everything."
-LADY MARY WORTLEY MONTAGU

"A word aptly spoken is like apples of gold in settings of silver"
(Proverbs 25:11 NIV).

Speaking the truth obviously means speaking what is conformable to fact; truthful, genuine, honest, and right. A lot of people, for various reasons can fall in the trap of speaking untruthful, whether they've read it, heard it, or even witnessed it. We should check ourselves instantaneously for the truth in anything we *hear, see, speak* or *do.*

Do you ever wonder how much of anything that is said or done is really true? Long ago I heard someone say, *"If you say a lie enough times, you'll believe it to be true."* The driving force behind this is repetition. How true this is and the power it propels. It's impossible to save the world from lying about certain issues, but what we can do, is start with where we are. Speaking truthful with repetition can assure us and our children protection. Yes, our words can *protect* us, and *preserve* us from harm, injury, or attack.

Truthful words can also guard, shield, safeguard, defend, and shelter.

In "guarding," we protect with extreme care and watchfulness against actual or potential harm. Parents do this well when protecting their children from the bullies at school or just plain forward children. My grandson had fallen on the tile when he was learning to walk and hurt his front teeth. Since there was damage, the teeth turned a darker color than his other teeth. By the time he started school, my daughter had spoken the truth to him about his baby teeth, assuring him that they would fall out and reveal two beautiful white front teeth. When questioned by other kids why his teeth were different, he'd intrigue them with his story and emphasized on the nice ending. Her true words served as a guard for her son.

"Shield" suggests an even stronger definition than protect, in which something is placed between that which is to be protected and the impending source of harm. Parents don't have to be overly protective in shielding their children from harm, disappointments or failures, if they speak the truth to them. Preparing them for the future starts with the truth in the present. By great confidence, their words serve as their shield.

"Safeguarding" implies that harm is not yet present and may even be remote, but that planning against its eventuality is prudent and farseeing. Smart parents not only safeguard their children against illness or lack, but also from the wrong words spoken around them. William Hazlitt says, *"Words are the only thing that lasts forever."* Then, I consider words to be an inheritance. So there you have it, safeguard your children against the future war of the words, by leaving the truth in their hearts.

"Defend" is a very interesting word, which emphasizes present harm and means to protect by use of force or other countermeasures. Here, we are talking about forceful words, not physical force. Every child must learn to defend himself, when necessary, from aggression of other children. It's okay to speak with strong forceful words as long as there is truth to them. A person who is truly confident of his strength, character and speech, does not need to parade it. This truly wise person does not look for chances to prove he's wise; in being resourceful, he can find his way out of any physical fight or an argument. On the same note, in being a person of endurance, he can take verbal abuse without retaliating. When I think on my father's words, they still make me giggle,

"Honey, just remember, there are the wise and the otherwise."

"Shelter" means to protect by offering or simply being a place of refuge or safety. This type of protection usually applies to providing cover. As a young child, I recall running into my grandmother's arms as her words sheltered me from the immediate harm and transformed my heart into a safety zone. One need only look at the truth behind one's words to know that which one protects, tends to be secure and safe.

Even if a small majority concerned themselves with the damage that curse words do, then it's a step forward towards demolishing the works they birth. This generation needs people who can demonstrate clearly (making it a lifestyle) how to live a full and a successful life by the words they speak. If they had us apply and fill out applications for such a position, would you be willing to be one of them? In all honestly, I believe it is our part in life to tell the truth, be fair and try to live at peace with everyone.

"Here is your part: Tell the truth. Be fair. Live at peace with everyone" (Zechariah 8:16 LV).

"Instead we will lovingly follow the truth at all times—speaking truly, dealing truly, living truly" (Ephesians 4:15 LV).

CHAPTER THREE

Flowers

Blooming

"You can call me flower if you want." This line from the Disney movie *Bambi* was constantly quoted in our home when the kids were young. I think it fits this chapter to a tee. After reading this *you* might want to be called "Flower."

To "bloom" is to reach a time of vigor, freshness, and beauty. "Vigor" means strength and energy. Bloom can also mean to shine with health or to glow, but in flowers or plant life it means to grow or flourish. Yes, you can call me flower if you want. What flower doesn't feel strength and energy, freshness and beauty, and shine and glow for everyone to see?

How many of us have heard the term *late bloomer*? The word seems to self define itself, so maybe an *on-time bloomer* is the one who attains full development of his abilities at the proper time they were intended for. I think we would all agree that we would rather be known as an *on-time bloomer* rather than a *late bloomer*, right? So, with this understanding, we as parents would all desire for our children to come into bloom attaining full development of his or her abilities, at their appointed time. The problem is; we don't always know when that may be. Agree? So, in reality, maybe there is no such thing as a late bloomer. It has been said, there is a time for everything.

As a natural flower is planted, watered, fertilized and taken care of properly, it is within its ability to bloom even though at times it will encounter resistance with the weather, the seasons and even the soil. Does anyone remember seeing the birth of a plant breaking through concrete to bear itself of its ability? This kind of visual helps me focus on passion, desire and purpose. Without hesitation, this plant did its thing and who's to say that it didn't have any sense at all.

Let's play a bit with our imaginations, okay? Imagine a plant could talk. Papa plant would ask the young sprout, *"What took you so long in blooming?"*

Knowing in his knower, the young one replied, *"Papa, the weather was so harsh this time around. Rain wasn't sufficient, extreme cold and hot days took turns sneaking up without warning and the sun hid itself behind shadowy clouds. Even the seasons were not favoring me, they left me behind, and the soil was as hard as a rock, my roots found no comfort in stretching to find food."*

"Little bud," Papa plant responded, *"Listen well as we examine our abilities. As a plant, we are an organized living body deriving our sustenance from the inorganic world, generally adhering to another body, and drawing from it some of its nourishment, and having the power to multiply ourselves."* Papa plant continued, *"Since birth you had in you the seed to multiply, therefore your only job is to do so. All you need is within your own ability. Excuses will kill your ability and therefore you will cease to exist. Believing in who you are and believing in what is in you, is the key to your survival."*

Okay, that was cute, huh? Now, applying it to us, what can we learn? In putting the excuses in two categories, it might be funny, but it will make sense. I'll humor you.

<u>Excuses of Little Sprout</u>	<u>Excuses of Human Sprouts (us)</u>
1. Weather	1. Whether (to do or not to do)

The forces that collectively constitute the weather; especially, cold, wind, rain, or other inclement influences, have a phenomenal effect on plants and animals. If we allow these elements to take precedence in our life then they'll create a perfect residence for laziness, procrastination, and lost hope. *"As long as the earth endures, seedtime and harvest, cold and heat, summer and winter, day and night will never cease"* (Genesis 8:22 NIV). We should not use what God created as an excuse to not perform our part in flourishing. All of the above elements and seasons are here to stay, our part is to be fruitful and multiply ourselves through our children.

2. Seasons 2. Reasons

Seasons/reasons occur or come with peculiar appropriateness and fit perfectly with the needs of the moment, character and occasion. Since reason is often applied to a motive, we should take caution that it doesn't become an excuse for missing the moment in the season that can change our life. *"There is a time for everything and a season for every activity under heaven"* (Ecclesiastes 3:1 NIV).

3. Soil 3. Soul (heart)

Soil is a place or condition favorable to growth, so is our Soul. The soil, as well as the soul, may respond differently towards a seed being sown, depending on the condition of the soil/soul. In Luke 8:5, a farmer was dealing with four types of soils. His job, no less than ours, is to scatter seed, but his goal is to get as much seed as possible to take root in good soil. Likewise, we will come across some shallow, rocky and thorny soils/souls, but we should let it not be an excuse which will keep us from sowing; for much seed is bound to fall on fertile soil/souls growing and producing a crop one hundred times as large as we planted.

Humans, as well as plants, are an organized living body in general adhering (stick fast or together) to another body. Other bodies we could adhere to could be our family, a mentor, a teacher, or a leader. This is where we can draw nourishment (wisdom, knowledge, understanding, encouragement, and support) to help in our growth and maturity as we multiply and leave valuable seed for the next generation of bloomers.

"Lives of great men all remind us
we can make our lives sublime.

And, departing, leave behind us,
footprints on the sands of time."
-HENRY WADSWORTH LONGFELLOW

"Sublime" is quite a special word, which means noble, inspiring awe or majestic. How amazing that many extraordinary men and women of the past have left us nuggets of gold pertaining to our abilities and the seeds of greatness within us. Mr. Zig Ziglar, one of my favorite writers of this era, believes that *man is endowed with seeds of greatness, designed for great accomplishments, and engineered for success.* I totally agree!

Unquestionably, Ralph Waldo Emerson, a widely known American essayist and poet of the 1800's, was on the same page with this quote, *"It's true—What lies behind us and what lies before us are tiny matters compared to what lies within us."* Never forget that you are the only one who can use your ability. It is an awesome responsibility. Go for it!

Interestingly, a flower is produced by a *natural process*, meaning, it is not artificial. Likewise, our valuable words are a natural process that the younger generation needs to reach their state of greatness. Nature itself is extraordinary—as it surrounds us, do we really take time to stop and smell the roses? What I mean by this is that lessons upon lessons are in nature itself, not for the mere existence of nature, but also for the existence of mans' being and character. Earlier, we noted the importance of building good character in our children. It takes good character to build good character. Good character builds a good reputation influencing and fueling a high quality-kind of ability.

A familiar parallel term of the word *bloom* is "to flower," which takes a beautiful meaning when applied to a person. *To flower,* gives rise to reaching the best period or thing or most vigorous stage of flourishing in a person's life. From this moment on, when you read about flowers, think about yourself. If a flower can bloom and flourish, so can you.

If you were to be a flower, which would you choose? It's kind of like choosing a dog for your pet. Many people believe that most four legged pets resemble their two legged masters. Let's see, I've seen flowers that are very beautiful and very fragrant. Paging through flower books and magazines, I've found flowers that take lots of abuse and still flourish. Then, there's some that are as delicate as a moth, some that only like full sun and others that are bashful and open only at night. One flower is even referred to as a *bright blessing.* Being a good food source for butterflies, deterring bugs, having culinary or medical uses or being a charming vegetable garden companion, is most interesting even for a flower. These are just a few of the many characteristics and kinds of flowers. I can easily imagine faces on these flowers of people that I know, can you?

Children take their projects very personal. One spring, for a *Mother's Day* project, I supplied different kinds of silk flowers for each child to choose for their craft. Before putting them in small vases, the children glued a photo of their smiling face in the center of their flower. Asking one child why she chose the sunflower, she replied, *"Because my mom calls me her sunshine."* In her mind, she related the sunflower to the sun, creating a vision of her mother's compliment to her.

Another child chose a red rose confirming that her mom always tells her she's as pretty as a rose. There was no doubt about it—this child was definitely pretty. A bit later, turning to a five year old blond-haired boy, I asked him why he had picked the daisy. Most proudly he responded, *"Because I like it when it stops at 'She loves me.'"* Then it came to me, *"She loves me, she loves me not. She loves me, she loves me not. She loves me!"*

Then last but not least, one cutie asked if I could help her find a marigold. Selecting it from the colorful pile of other flowers, I asked her why she wanted that particular one. As her smile formed two deep dimples, she answered, *"Well, my mom's name is Mary and she has a heart of gold."* Children can naturally apply themselves into a world of imagination, when it comes to pretending. In doing so, they can easily relate to the beauty and simplicity of life just being something else.

More than a thousand flowers have been named and classified with such descriptions as sweet, fine, silky, colorful, graceful, healthy, strong, bright, healers, admirable, helpful, soothing, peaceful and much, much more. Have you ever wondered, *"Does the flower know its abilities?"* My personal answer is: *"Only a flower knows what a flower knows."* As any plant will know to do its thing, we too must know to do our thing. By the way, do we really know our abilities? Do we know what our thing is to do?

As anyone who loves gardening knows; a plant's four major problems can be: (1) Not enough sunshine; (2) Overwatering; (3) Over fertilizing or not fertilizing at all; (4) Pots are too small. Okay, for us so called flowers, let's examine these problems and see how they apply to us.

We need sunshine to grow and flourish. The great and powerful sun, with its distance from the earth of about 93 million miles, has its purpose for existing—to sustain life providing heat and light. Experts say that we should all get a little sunshine whenever possible. The cute kid's song that comes to mind, *"You are my Sunshine,"* fits the definition of *sunshine* when referring to such words as warm, pleasant, bright, and cheerful. Everyone deserves to have a *Sunshine* in their life.

How can we get over watered? As we all know, water (H2O) is essential for all life. My dad made sure I understood that there are two sides to every action; the good and the bad. Applying this principle, we see that excessive water will definitely drown most plants/life. It takes more water to make things watery, and the same applies to words. Too many words can cause our speech to become diluted, resulting in either weakening, or overdoing what's being communicated. Our words to others should aim to help, encourage and support without lacking the full ability and power behind what they are meant to accomplish. Well-watered words should make us full of life.

"If you're above water, you're out of trouble; if you're in deep water, you're in deep trouble; but if you hold water, you are logical and persistent." -WEBSTER

Over fertilizing is over feeding, *under fertilizing* is under feeding. One can't have a beautiful, healthy garden without proper nourishment. We must strive to be part of a rich, healthy and prosperous garden where unity is evident. A flower isn't just a flower to be a flower, yet it survives for purpose. Likewise, we are not just humans to be humans. We all have purpose for our existence. We must want to choose to live in a precious garden filled with rich and sweet fragrances, stunning colors, and unspeakable beauty where there's food source of all kinds, filled with charming companions that discourage the buggers in our lives while others aid in our health and culinary needs. All this is a great lesson to learn from one life form to another.

Our words also need the right fertilization, nourishment and care to develop into life-flowing words. We shouldn't hang out with weeds even if they're in the middle of your garden. Often we let the values and actions of others around us dictate our attitudes and behavior. At some point we have all made a wrong choice by wanting to be like everyone else. Even though the values of some of our friends might catch our attention, we must be careful not to let them pull us away from our well rooted plan.

Have you ever brought home a plant or a flower whose roots are all crammed in its original pot? Its survival depends on you carefully removing it from the small pot, untangling the roots and repotting it into a larger pot. Just imagine if our roots were all tangled up and crammed in a very small pot. In fact, the *root* of a plant is the portion underground that serves as support, draws food and water from the surrounding soil and stores food. All the sunshine, water and fertilizer will make no difference to any living form if the roots are not healthy. Once the root problem is taken care of, then the plant can *take root* (begins to grow, becoming firm, fixed and established). Interestingly the verb form of "root" means to lend support to someone or something or to give encouragement. If we continue with strong roots in our families, those same roots will put forth stronger roots in our children as we lend support and encourage them through life as they bloom to their fullest capacity. We must care for our roots, they support our life.

"You need to realize how important your words are. They set the boundaries of your life."

"You will never realize anything beyond the words you speak. You will never have anything beyond your own words."
-KENNETH E. HAGIN

CHAPTER FOUR

Trees

Foundation

The "foundation" is a basis upon which something stands or is supported, or as we already know; the roots. This word comes from the root word *found,* which means to lay the basis or groundwork of anything—literal or figurative. In drafting, I was able to see and familiarize myself with the *foundation plan* of a house or a building. It is most interesting that the supported factor of the foundation in any house, building, company, tree and even a family is the role of withstanding the trials and experiences of time.

The uniqueness of a tree has inspired many poets and writers attributing its strong foundation, strength, height and its roots in relation to the greatness of man. As you read some of these characteristics of a mighty creation—the tree—imagine how much greater of a creation you are.

From the moment a tree begins to grow, "form" and "plan" are in its very structure of existence. Likewise, from the moment a human begins to grow (in the womb), *form*, *plan,* and *purpose* are in its very structure of existence. Yes, we've had a purpose for living before we came out of the womb.

"I knew you before you were formed within your mother's womb" (Jeremiah 1:5 LV).

"Well-rooted" trees support a well-defined main stem (trunk) that dominates its form throughout its life cycle, later forming a number of equally important branches. Despite the fact that the roots in most plants are not exposed visually, the branches and the fruit will determine how strong a foundation it has; this holds true in our lives as well. Being *well-rooted* gives strong support to our bodies throughout our life as we also form our branches, of talents, abilities and gifts, all of which are of equal importance. As our branches mature, our fruit will grow. In all respect, trees and man are appointed to bear fruit. Will others know us by our fruit?

"Godly men are growing a tree that bears life-giving fruit" (Proverbs 11:30 LV).

The trunk of a tree "renews itself" every year. The bark insulates and protects the trunk and often shows characteristic cracks or falls off, leaving a smooth skin. Dare yourself the challenge of renewing yourself every year, whether spiritually, mentally, or physically. Sometimes we need to shake our yesterday off of ourselves in order to grow today. We should be honest in the estimate of ourselves, measuring our value by daily renewing ourselves.

"Don't copy the behavior and customs of this world, but be a new and different person with the newness in all you do and think" (Romans 12:2 LV).

"Our only concern should be to do better than we did yesterday. Step by step is the law of growth. God does not expect the acorn to be a mighty oak before it has been a sapling." -GEORGE E. CARPENTER

A tree has the power of "reproduction" and the power to renew itself from injuries, keeping itself going on and on with a stout heart. Man was created with an ability to reproduce, to be fruitful and to multiply. Our bodies are amazing healing machines that propel our determined hearts to keep on going.

"We have a responsibility here on earth, and we have already been equipped."

A tree can "overcome obstacles," split rocks apart, and even its roots travel far in the thirsty search for water. Okay, not all of us can split rocks apart, but overcoming obstacles are high on our list of challenges, not to mention how far we would go for a drink of water.

An obstacle is often an unrecognized opportunity. Our whole life is an obstacle course; we should run that we may obtain what is set before us.

It's amazing how a tree can "adjust" to circumstances and "endure" unending existence all on its own. Definitely, we can adjust to and endure circumstances of all sorts, though at times we may choose not to. Well, a tree has no choice; either change or die.

In a race, it is not the start that hurts, not even the long stretch, but it's when the goal is in sight that our heart, our nerves, our courage, and our muscles are pushed beyond human endurance, many times causing adjustment to our circumstances.

Every tree is "an individual," no two are alike, even when cut into boards from the same tree; each piece is as different as a human's fingerprints are from anyone else's in the world. Each one of us is a unique individual with a different form and plan for our lives, yet with one purpose—sowing our seed for tomorrow.

Purpose is individually given, manifested through unity, and harvested tomorrow.

Trees are "perennial" plants. Another name for perennial is *perpetual,* which means lasting or active through many years. How many of us can truly say that we can be perennial in our ways and life? Have you ever heard of perennial happiness? Many of us have heard or read stories that ended with, *"...and they lived happily ever after."* I'd call that a perpetual harvest of happiness. If we were truly convinced that all seed has the ability to produce a perpetual harvest, then we would take precautions on what kind of seed we are sowing today.

We should so live and labor in our time that what came to us as seed may go to the next generation as a blossom, and what came to us as a blossom may go to them as fruit. This is a perpetual harvest.

Have you ever witnessed kindergarteners imitating a tree? It's totally amusing to watch as they flamboyantly spread out their little arms, exhibiting their branches. In their minds they portray all trees as gigantic towers. In their marching, alone, reveals order, strength, and greatness, above all, life. Unaffected, these little ones act the part of a massive plant, too empowering for their little minds to even begin to understand, so we think. Then there's of course, the dialogue. It's a mystery in itself, how a child can mimic a tree while taking on the appearance of it from a picture in his/her mind. Yes, it's quite entertaining to see these little five year old actors, caricaturing their models and adding voices as they see fit. Suited with deep voices, and hovering over other smaller human trees, rehearsing such claims as, *"I'm a big monster tree and my branches are the longest."* Or maybe something like this, *"Come sit under my big branches and rest."* Picture a happy-looking tree, just hopping around with a big smile, singing happy little songs. Most of you were thinking of a palm tree, right? Well, growing up, most of us have seen talking trees, and maybe some of us are still seeing them with our small children in the homes, but have you ever wondered what it would be like to be a tree? Not a kindergarten tree, but a real tree? It is time for more fun.

In an earlier chapter, you were challenged to imagine what it would be like to be a flower of your choice. Now, what about a tree? What kind of tree would fascinate you enough to not mind being in his shoes, or rather in its roots? Better yet, what kind of tree would you say fits your type of personality?

When inspired by nature, it's wise to take notes, take pictures and take notice. Botanical gardens are breath-taking and fully packed with nature-lessons. Apart from being magnificent plants, trees freely inspire those who are mesmerized by their beauty. The beauty of a tree radiates in its surroundings.

This analogy teaches us something. Read on.

1). Trees always seem to be looking up.

Lesson: Sometimes we get distracted if we don't keep our eyes and heads up.

"When you're looking at the sun, you see no shadows."
-HELEN KELLER

***"When the outlook isn't good, try the up look—
it's always good."***-ZIG ZIGLAR

2). Trees have no fear-they just know to do what they were created to do.

Lesson: You are the only person on this planet earth that can use your abilities, talents and gifts.

***"One reason people never attempt new
things is their fear of failure."***

***"Do not wish to be anything but what you are,
and try to be that perfectly."***-ZIG ZIGLAR

3). A tree knows its purpose and lives it without doubt.

Lesson: We, like any tree, might look ordinary, but we've got extra-ordinary purpose.

***"You have within you all of the qualities and seeds
necessary for success and to fulfill purpose in your life."***

4). <u>No matter where a tree stands, it is unique because of what is within.</u>

Lesson: Within you are unspeakable opportunities ready to happen.

"What lies behind us and what lies before us are tiny matters compared to what lies within us."
-RALPH WALDO EMERSON

5). <u>Trees endure. Their goal is to live forever. They remain firm no matter what circumstances it encounters.</u>

Lesson: When you have a goal, a direction, or a plan the power of endurance is fueled from within.

"Endurance is the crowning quality"
-JAMES RUSSELL LOWELL

"...To achieve great things we must live as though we were never going to die."
-MARQUIS DE VAUVE-NARGUES

Fruitful

It stands to reason, that if we are to bear fruit, why not bear in abundance, producing amazing profitable results? Could it be because we were never told that we could, or believed that we could, or maybe we were never taught to do so? I want to encourage you and help you see what a magnificent person you are, and that your fruit will come in due season. First of all, believe in the God who created you, and last, but not least, believe in yourself.

If we were trees, we would probably learn to think out of the box, because what's in us is not just for us. For a tree to keep its wood to itself, would cause lack elsewhere. This concept is true for any part of the tree, the trunk, its roots, its branches, and of course its fruit; whether berries, pinecones, nuts or even its sweet fragrant flowers. What are we doing with our talents, gifts, abilities, time and even our finances? These are all fruits and all fruits have seed. Using wisely what we have to help ourselves, our families, friends and others that need our kind of fruit is fulfilling purpose. A seed, well planted, will produce in abundance with profitable results which will reveal the plant (person) behind the fruit.

"You would not think any duty small if you yourself were great." -GEORGE MACDONALD

Countless physicians, professionals and experts in all sorts of fields and trades are daily supplying to numerous needs around the globe. With all due respect, each and every one of us should be bearing fruit and supplying to one another, regardless of profession. Maybe some of us find it a bit difficult pin-pointing what it is that we have to supply or offer to another, then, perhaps, we should try picturing ourselves as a living and fruitful tree.

Only a tree expert can cite the pedigree values and composition of most trees and of the millions of variety. Following are a few that caught my attention. I assure you, these trees along with us, were created with purpose. This chapter is not only for us to learn about trees, but to capture something about ourselves.

Interestingly, the Cypress tree provides man with precious *medicine.* I believe that a lot of us are walking prescriptions whether we know it or not. Think about it, has anyone ever made this comment, *"I feel much better now."* after seeing or talking to you? How about at the hospital, the many who feel a burst of energy after a touch, a loving word or just the presence of someone being there? Remember the story of the little boy and the grandpa in the hospital? Now, that was a big dose of healthy medicine administered by a child. A wise king once wrote, *"A faithful friend is the medicine of life."*

The Scotch pine, a gigantic 120 foot tall evergreen is essential in *respiratory* ailments. *"You're a breath of fresh air."* This saying, in most cases, is used in reference to making a difference in someone's day. Some of you are just that, making someone's day special, as if you were a drop of medicine. Some of us, with just the right words can bring calmness, allowing others to believe everything is going to be okay. With this kind of feeling, surely anyone can breathe better. Respiratory, as well as many other ailments can lead to serious conditions requiring medical attention, yet we can be the first in helping with wise words full of life, being a breath of fresh air to another person.

How nice if we were all as a 100 foot tall Ylang-ylang tree, giving others a feeling of great happiness or well-being. This tree doesn't hold a candle to grandchildren. Any grandparent will agree that a grandchild can truly bring great happiness along with a feeling of extra well-being when they are around. At some point, you will be that surrounding happiness that a friend might need or a stranger will feel.

Though from a small tree, the Frankincense's oil is used on wounds and ulcers. No matter how small we are, we can be useful if we avail ourselves. This reminds me of the many wounds (scrapes, scratches, and broken hearts), that felt better after a simple kiss during the many years as a young mother, a kindergarten teacher and now as a grandmother. As far as ulcers go, the right medication together with the right TLC (tender loving care), serves as a dual remedy. Don't pass up on an opportunity to stay with someone for a while until they feel better. How awesome it would be to read on a prescription, *"Take the recommended dosage together with the company of one who cares. Repeat as needed."*

The evergreen Mandarin tree has fragrant flowers, and reaches heights of twenty feet. Its fruit's loose skin yields oil that benefits insomnia. Okay, I imagine this kind of tree as a women, mom or grandma, rocking a child to sleep, or just rocking for the sake of rocking. I remember my grandma's perfume as she rocked me on her oversized rocker until I fell asleep, or the memory of my mother coming into my room at night after a bad dream, and sitting with me until I fell asleep again. With this, I'm sure many grandmas could have easily fit the name, Mandarin.

The fast growing Eucalyptus tree reaches heights of 300 to 400 feet. Its oil aids in clearing the head. Of course, no one grows to 400 feet, except maybe the hulk, but we won't talk comics, okay? Many times I've had to take long walks to clear my head. It works. The right cup of tea, the right people, the right music and even the right book can all help in clearing the head from nonsense or just a heavy load. The eucalyptus tree can hold no candle to some of you. How about helping someone clear their heads from a busy day by offering them your time as a seed?

Of the million of trees in this world, whether tall, short, big, small, or strong, they all have purpose. Trees, as well as humans were created to provide—in doing so—we have to learn to survive. Our past and the present provide us with techniques for our survival. Much wisdom has gone into words already spoken for our benefit, and together with what is done and spoken now—in the present—we have what it takes to survive.

"The Wisdom of the Wise and the Experience of the Ages may be Preserved by Quotations."
-ISAAC D'ISRAELI

The words we speak give value to our existence, not merely by what we accumulated on our own, but by what lives on after we are gone. So, it's been said, the sum total of our existence is made up of what we forward to others, as an expression of what is important to us. The question is: What is important to you? Have you ever thought of what your children are passing on to their children, and their children to theirs? The key to help you think of this in realistic form is to think of your children in the future, as adults.

The following quote, referring to a tree, holds true for man as well: *"A tree is known by the kind of fruit it produces"* (Matthew 7:20 LV). We are known by what type of fruit we produce. Others can determine what we are like by looking at what our life generates. Bear in mind, what we do, or say speaks volumes about us; even in the future through our own seed.

Here Henri J.M. Nouwen, I believe, understood the truth of bearing fruit: *"Our doing brings success, but our being bears fruit. The great paradox of our lives is that we are often concerned about what we do or still can do, but we are most likely to be remembered for whom we were."*

We've all heard the saying, *"the fruit does not fall far from the tree."* We bear what is in us as we continue to grow, and the harvest that we produce will let everyone know whether or not we are real or fake. Can we honestly say that we can confirm the authenticity of what we are being taught? Remember, in a previous chapter we read, *"Be honest in your estimate of yourself, measuring your value."* The real *you* is authentic. Let your fruit confirm the real *you*. This reminds me of how unique a child is, in the fact, that they can pretty much pick up what is real and what is fake in a person. In most cases, a child will draw to an adult that likes children, relying only on inner discernment. Even a baby can spot a baby lover from afar with giggles and a tender smile. And just as well, I'm sure every mother has witnessed their baby refraining from smiling to a not-so-loveable person. And there's another way that a fake can be detected, that is in stamps. Postage stamps have a phosphorescent dye that is picked up by an ultraviolet light that aids in sorting out fake stamps on mail sent through the post office. Well, we certainly aren't stamps, and we can't stay babies all of our life, so let's move on and sow good seed so that we can all have good fruit and be real about our lives. It's as easy as that, because when we're gone, we're gone! Our seeds stay for the future.

And in closing, as Secretary Stanton said at Abraham Lincoln's death, *"Now he belongs to the ages."* Our words are eternal. After we're gone, our words belong to the age of the future. Let's make them worthwhile and lasting for many ages to come!

"We judge ourselves by what we feel capable of doing, while others judge us by what we have already done."
-HENRY WADSWORTH LONGFELLOW

Branches

"Blessed is the man that delights and walks in the law of the Lord and meditates day and night, He shall be like a tree planted by the rivers of water, bearing forth his fruit in his season, his leaf shall not wither; and all they do shall prosper"
(Psalms 1:1-3).

Suppose you were a giant tree with many branches extending from your main body. Well, in a way we are. I've seen some very impressive family trees with many branches and deep roots that have nourished many dreams up-line from the same stock. Unlike trees, with a far longer life span than ours and far much stronger, our existence can outlive anything through the *words* we have spoken from generation to generation.

Do you agree that one of the greatest forces in the natural world is *growth*? I believe that a tree is the noblest example of that force. I also believe that Love is the #1 example where without growth it will cease to live or continue, but as long as growth has a place, it can outlive time, therefore becoming the greatest ultimate force in the natural world. I will be introducing "Love" in the last chapter of this book, but for now, let me impress you with some simple, yet specific facts as we reflect on the life of a tree versus our life. As you read these particular points, see yourself unstoppable as you live up to your potential with purpose.

A tree springs up from a seed, and soars skyward a hundred feet or more. It draws up water against gravity spreading with splendor its boughs and twigs, yet living to the outermost leaf.

"Living to the outermost leaf," seems to mean caring what kind of fruit each branch produces. That's a lot like families. The parents live to give life and take honor and pride when they see a fruitful child (branch) sprout, and produce fruit, and as we all know, fruit has seeds.

"Everything comes from a seed."

Just as a tree, we sprouted from a *seed*. Though most of us don't grow as tall as a tree, but we do "soar." In referring to our character growth, the following synonyms of the word *soar* would be quite impressive to see in our little sprouts as they *rise, arise, tower, rocket, aspire, and aim* into the future. All children, as well as you and I, were born with seeds of greatness in us that inspires us to want to soar into life; as high as life can take us. Our children need to be nourished in a strong healthy way, especially through the words we speak to them as they're growing up. The right words will fuel their dreams, where they too, can live to their fullest potential.

Many times we seem to go against the flow in life. In most cases, if we strongly believe in ourselves, we'll be determined to survive in this busy world. No matter how tough life might get, we have the ability to keep on going. It is the instinct within that came with our life when we were created with purpose. Every kind of life has within itself an instinct to survive. In tropical regions, you'll see the palm tree standing tall and upright, but as you get closer to the shoreline, you'll see the leaning ones that withstood the strong winds and survived.

"Nothing is impossible: there are ways which lead to everything; and if we have sufficient will, we should always have sufficient means."
-FRANCOIS DE LA ROCHEFOUCAULD

"If a plant had a brain," said Darwin, *"it would lie in its roots."* If only we could see deep into the earth as a plant seeks to find water, as it dodges obstacles, prying through what would seem impossible to penetrate. Nevertheless, its delicate root tips penetrate the soil in a spiral motion. When in contact with an obstacle, such as a rock, it may avoid it or overcome it. The plant has the capability of raising or lifting an obstacle aside, or even cracking it open, by dissolving it with acids that it secretes. Even in a drought, a grand old tree will find drink enough to keep alive in the film of moisture that clings to every grain of soil. A plant will go to the extremes to survive, because it was created to do so.

Ever wonder what kind of roots you're connected to? As mentioned earlier, some of our *roots* are tied to words, and when something is tied, it has limitations. There are also root words left for us that fuel and fire the imagination of our future dreams and goals. Some of us already have strong roots, so we must continue our journey building upon that foundation in order for our children to move into the future with confidence.

Like a mirror image of the tree above, the underground growth has first a taproot corresponding to the trunk, then huge primary branches. It is said, the best way to water a trees is under the outermost branches. Coming from a family of eleven children, it was obvious that my mother and father watered and nourished the family branches directly above them with equal attention. A tree waters all of itself, not just parts of it. The same goes with parents, we need to nourish every part of our child—his mind soul and body.

With the passing years, I began to understand that the time and money my parents spent on each of us was an investment in *our* future. It wasn't so much about them as it was for us. Making a successful life for ourselves was their harvest from the seeds they've sown. Investing in our children, is investing in the future. This type of investment is the ultimate investment of all times.

It's amazing that a tree has no set limit to its size or age. Its aim is to keep growing and branching out. I'm sure it didn't questioned itself, "*Why me*?" Our children should be allowed to dream *big*, aiming for greatness in their generation. My daughter, from a very young age, knew and understood this concept, and to this day, there is no limit to what she can believe for. Most trees' main purpose is to be used for something, whether food, furniture, medicine, housing, toys, canopy of shade or to simply go down in history. In our branching out, using our time, talents, abilities, finances, and efforts, we too can be used to benefit mankind as well as ourselves. Making a difference in life, using our seeds of greatness within us, will leave strong roots for the future. Interestingly enough, a tree is one part of nature that can help us stay focused and inspire us to be all we have been created to be.

A Tree is More Than a Tree

A Tree is more than man can see,
Infused with life and destiny.
Such mysteries within its core,
Clearly reveals what once it bore.

What King has nature ever crowned,
With boughs of spendor all around?
Humbled Kingdom without a throne,
Flows richly in treasures of own.

Man's convinced there's hope for a tree,
If cut down, new sprouts will be.
If roots grow old beneath the ground,
The stump will die without a sound.

With scent of water, I'll burst forth,
Reviving life with endless worth.
A tree is more than just a tree,
When it expresses God's Glory.
-MAE

CHAPTER FIVE

Moon

Night Light

Above in darkness, a light so shines,
As her beauty captures restless minds.
Her provision shines brighter at night,
When reflecting off the greatest light.

The gazes of awe from time gone by,
Were memories fleeting in the sky.
The moon though one is never alone,
The lovers of time claim her their own.

Her beauty seen only in distance,
No light will shine if in its entrance.
It's best to admire her from afar,
Imagine her as your priceless star.
-Mae

The "moon" serves of its life. How interesting. Does mankind serve of his life? What's in our life to offer? First, let's see what the moon offers of itself.

We've all seen how beautiful the moon is on a clear night, when all is quiet and peaceful. It seems to invite thoughts to wander off into a land of deep imagination. We're all fascinated by the distance of this great night light in the sky. Yet, it's not a light at all, but a reflection upon its outer core from the greatest star of all—the sun. I wonder, what can reflect upon *us,* causing *us* to be more than just ordinary?

Was it the moon's purpose to shine at night, giving light for lovers, hunters, and refugees? Was it her purpose to be arranged as a centerpiece of myths, monuments and religions? Was it in her purpose to be a presence and influence on our earth's natural and astronomical order? Was it part of her purpose to be the dominant timekeeper for us? Was it her purpose to be classified as a target for the telescope, pointing astronomers and for the rocket, steering astronauts into space? Was it in her purpose to be a source of inspiration for writers, artists, dreamers and lovers? The answer is *yes* to all of the above. Just as the moon was created to be a moon, what it does within its purpose is the greatest of all gifts; it is there that she gives of herself.

Some of us think that we are meant to do one thing only and nothing more. Many of us would be surprised to know of the many ways we can make a difference for others if we just stop thinking only of ourselves, or on titles that we have worked so hard to earn. What can we learn from the moon? Well, although, the moon is not a human, we can still learn how multi-tasking within our own purpose can touch more lives than we'll ever know. When we think out of the box, we can see past the four walls of ourselves, we can even expand our borders of creativity! Wow! Imagine that! One single person has so much to offer the world, and yet it's possible that that one person is probably the only one that doesn't know it! How sad. This is a really good time for you to examine yourself. Ok?

Take a break (just a short one, please). Relax. Take a deep breath (let it out). Ask yourself the following questions: Who are you? What are you? What things do you like to do? What are your hobbies? What are your talents? What are your gifts? What are you able and capable of doing for others?

Now, close your eyes for about a minute and think about your answers.

Make the time to search yourself, until you can see and identify the seeds of greatness deep within you. Write down what you would like to do. Check your list and add to it when needed. Don't forget that you are more than just a body. You are living and walking provider for the future, whether what you do is for today, tomorrow or for much later into the future. Ok?

In the large state of Texas, as a child, I recall one very dark evening when we got a flat tire in the middle of *no-where* land. Not having a flash light, made it extremely difficult for Dad to see while trying to change the tire. Removing the nuts and bolts from the wheel, he placed them on the turned-over hub cap. At one point of frustration he accidentally kicked the cap and the nuts and bolts all rolled under the car. Almost impossible to see, he reached under the car to retrieve the parts, only to find a hand full of small rocks and pebbles. His grumbling and clanging of tools was interrupted by a set of headlights approaching us from afar. Not knowing whether to work faster or try to wave for help, he just continued working, cautiously looking up every second or two. Within a short time a car pulled up and asked if we needed help. With his flash light and his kindness in helping, we were soon on our way home. Upon leaving he introduced himself saying he was the owner of the hotel in the next town and invited us to visit some time. Though he was a Hotel Owner by title, that night he was our *night light*.

The main definition of *light*, as we all know it to be, is the electromagnetic radiation that can be perceived by the normal eye. There's another kind of light that glows from *us*; the *light of our life*. Light, given the fact that there are many sources of it, is a most variable subject to ponder on. For instance, when you hear the word *light*, what pictures run through your mind? I see a candle, a light bulb, a street light, the sun, the moon, glow sticks and even lightening bugs. I can even picture a smile from my own grandchildren. Your mind might paint many more pictures, but what we see is that *light* is a good thing. When we refer to someone as the light of our life, we are expressing a positive trait in that person. In the Bible we are all called to be *light*.

Speaking of *light*, some of us *light-hearted* people, free from troubles or cares can choose to spread lots of *light* to others, brightening up their day with merely our presence. Some of us shed *light* on a specific matter with our words, being as a beacon to many. Beacon is defined as a *light* for warning or guiding. Is this not what we are to be for our children and families? Outlining *light* as a noun, it expresses *an outstanding person*.

Furthermore, "light" is a most interesting element; no matter how dim or bright, small or large, in or out, it is still *light*. Our children might start out as small lights, but other big lights can light their way into the future. We are not called to be a *light,* hidden from the world, but to be used as a tool for lighting up the present and the future regardless how bright we shine, or how small we may seem.

"You are the world's light—a city on a hill, glowing in the night for all to see. Don't hide your light! Let it shine for all; let your good deeds glow for all to see, so that they will praise your heavenly Father" (Matthew 5:14-16 LV).

In the above verse, we are compared to a city on a hill, where its light can be seen for miles at night. At times we might hide our light without realizing. Some of us may not speak or act when we should; denying the light within to be exposed. When I worked around children, whether in public schools or Sunday school, every morning I would do a quick-check on the children as they entered the class. *"Did you put on your smile, today? Did you turn on your listening ears? Did you turn on your little light?"* What if we did a daily check on ourselves before starting out on our busy day? Instead of singing, *"Hi ho, hi ho, it's off to work I go..."* try, *"This little light of mine, I'm gonna let it shine...let it shine, let it shine, let it shine."*

Two synonyms of light; *illuminate* and *enlighten,* enrich the definition of *light* as applied to us. The unfolding of our words gives light to those around us. In seeing ourselves and our children as *light* by the words we speak, let's apply the principles of what light does:

First, light *exposes* what is present.

Second, light *energizes* the growth potential of what's alive.

Third, light *attracts* in a single direction what it energizes toward growth.

So in other words, we, as light, can dispel darkness, sparking growth, and positively directing the flow of life. To be the kind of *light* that this world needs requires change. Can *we* make a difference in this world? The answer is *YES!* We must all start with ourselves and our families.

Many of us, as children, have shined a flashlight into the sky at night and wondered how far the light would travel. Later in learning that light travels in a straight line into space at the speed of roughly 186,000 miles per second, made me wonder how fast do our words travel if they last forever? Maybe the light from a flashlight will die out at some point, but our words will remain eternal. Where is it that our words are taking us? Are we moving in the right direction? We might never know exactly where or how our words have an effect on our future, but it is possible to feel and know that we are on the right track and moving forward.

"I find the great thing in this world is not so much where we stand, as in what direction we are moving."
-OLIVER WENDELL

Occasionally, we become accustomed to the shadows that hide the patterns and practices of our lives. Then in some light, they are exposed or revealed, whether through our children's behavior or by those around about us. It's always easier to remain the same than to cause a change. In all honesty, when challenged by light to change our lives, most would rather live in darkness. We must believe that *change* is good and that we *can* make a difference. Remember, fear of change is always a brake on progress. Living without change is the same as life without light. We need to know when to let go, so change can take over.

"Darkness" as not only a state of not receiving, reflecting, transmitting, or radiating light of any kind; it defines a stage of gloom or hopelessness as well as arising from or showing evil traits. Being kept in the dark means there is not a clear understanding or knowledge of something. *Being a light* and *being in the light* is the way to go, if you want your children and their children to continue in the future. *"My people are destroyed from lack of knowledge"* (Hosea 4:6 NIV). We must all be willing and ready to learn and change in order for life to go on. Don't believe this saying; *"What you don't know won't hurt you."* Life is for us to learn from, whether it's now, later or from the past. Promoting and supervising the mental and moral growth of our children creates vision in their lives. Man must have vision to survive! *Light* is also that which makes vision possible. What's your *vision*? What about your goals? Can you see them clearly? *"Where there is no vision, the people perish"* (Proverbs 29:18 KJV).

"Having a goal is a state of happiness." –E.J. BARTEK

In our home growing up, my dad was big on not accepting the words *"I can't do that"*, or *"I don't like it."* He would ask, *"How do you know if you can't do something, or if you don't like something, if you haven't tried it before?"* It is important for us to teach our children to think and try things for themselves and not rely on other's opinions. A fine example I recall, as a young girl, was that I did not like pecan pie, because of the vivid description in the making of them that was told to me by another child. On the other hand, it was my dad's favorite pie. One day he asked if I wanted a piece of his pie. I quickly answered, *"No, thank you. I don't like it."* He proceeded to ask me why. (I'm sure he was wondering why anyone in their right mind couldn't possibly like pecan pie.) Once again, I answered, *"I don't know, I just don't like it."* I was hoping he would just drop the whole subject and enjoy his pie in peace, but he wasn't ready to give it up,

"Have you ever tried it?" he asked.

"No, but I already know I don't like it," I answered quickly. Before he asked again, I decided to give him the whole scoop of why I did not like pecan pie. (I will spare you the details, or else I'll be blamed for you not liking pecan pie.)

Anyway, a bit disappointed at my reason for not liking pecan pie, he sternly questioned me, *"You don't like pecan pie because someone else didn't like pecan pie? And you believed her? Honey, I wish I would have spoken to you before this person did, because if you would have believed me, you would be eating pecan pie right now. So just try it, then, you'll see what* ***you*** *believe to be true about pecan pie."*

I tried it. *"Now, I like pecan pie!"* Since pecan pie was my dad's favorite; when I was old enough, I learned to make them especially for him. Imagine how many times I would have missed in blessing my dad if I had never learned the truth about the making of pecan pies.

"No one knows what it is that he can do 'til he tries."
-PUBLILIUS SYRUS

It's a healthy routine to point out the qualities in our children as a reminder and as an encouragement to them. Children need to be aware of their abilities and talents in learning to focus on their potential. Our words will fuel their being and even their potential. We should never limit our children to what they can do. Life is too short to spend it on one thing alone and nothing more. The more you're open in teaching your child, the more opportunities he or she may have in life. Many times, we ourselves are so much more than we think we are. Even our own potential is meaningless if we are unaware of it. Few of us have an awareness of how precious and valuable we are. Even the least motivated person possesses the power and the right to choose a life full of abundance.

Nurturing our children means that we are training, caring and bringing them up according to what they were created to be. Of course this is based totally on their own talents, abilities and skills, *not* ours. As we come to recognize their talents and abilities, then we will nourish those gifts. Nourishing our child's gifts means that we have the responsibility to feed and provide them with the things needed for life and growth.

Acquiring abilities and skills for loving children could very well lean towards the fact of being the oldest daughter of eleven children or maybe just observing other care givers in my family. Through the many years, I was told that I would be a good mommy some day. The many times I recall playing school with my younger brothers and sisters, and making copies of color sheets over my glass window, could have fueled my desire to become a teacher? Even back then, as a pretend teacher, with pretend students, I heard, *"You are a nice teacher."* A child's playground is the beginning of their future.

Watching both my parents in the kitchen, at different times, conditioned me to believe that, anybody could cook. Even the majority of my brothers profited from this lifestyle. We didn't cook because Mom or Dad told us to, it was because we saw it being done regularly and casually by them both. Compliments were as common as good manners in our house. Whether we cooked, sewed, gardened, cleaned or whatever; there was always a *"thank-you"* or *"that was nice."*

Mother and Father were both very creative. Aside from being a hard worker, my dad worked with leather. Seeing him sketch out his designs, then work with his hands to create his masterpieces, fed my interest and desire to work with my hands. In the same manner, my mother, a seamstress, designed and created clothes for us. Today, I can look back and see how each one of my brothers and sisters acquired their talents and gifts. Even before we were taught *art* in school, we were learning how to draw and create amazing things at home. By the time *Home Economics* was offered in school, we were already being prepared at home with life skills. Many of our own gifts, talents and abilities have been passed down to our own children, but only *they* can do with them what *they* can do. Recognizing our own purpose is the road to a perfect plan for our lives, it's not too high or too low. It's not too wide or too narrow and it's not too easy and not too hard. It's perfect!

"No bird soars too high, if he soars with his own wings"
-WILLIAM BLAKE

We've all heard of a "Jack of all Trades." I'm sure there are a lot of them, whereas some might very well be you and I. Though we do many things well, we all have to focus on our strongest skill and talent, and help our children to do as well. We as parents or guardians have an awesome opportunity and responsibility in directing them. All the qualities acquired while growing up are seeds deposited in them from an early age. Our words of encouragement and approval are forms of fuel that help build up the faith needed to propel these gifts and talents into action. Even though some things will be done better than others, we just have to see our young ones in the playground of learning life skills through us, our words and our actions. Some *Jack of all Trades* can sing, dance, sew, draw, paint, write, fly, sail, build, design, care, speak, act, etc.

Don't be surprised when you see your sons or daughters doing all of the above. Most humans have the capability to multi-function. Whatever God put in your child as gifts and talents, He is faithful to complete. I didn't have to compete with my mother and have eleven children to love children, nor acquire a "Chef's" degree to feed people in my own home. Even a fashion designer greatly benefited from my talent and skills of designing clothes for his company. I've had the honor and privilege of teaching children, even before I was a school teacher. Even my prayers, friendship and encouragement to others have healed broken hearts and even a sick body, and yet, I am definitely not a medical Doctor, by no means nor title.

Parents, grandparents and teachers, please compliment a child when needed. Your very words will fuel that talent and ability, whether now or later. Even if a child's work or accomplishments are not much to compare to another, we still must see the work for what it is worth by the doer. When my grandchildren first began to draw pictures for me, their masterpieces were unrecognizable. I was careful not to insult their ability. At times, thinking that a dog was a cat, or a person was a pumpkin, or even a flower was a tree, I'd compliment them first by saying, *"Wow this is really good, you draw so beautifully, I love the colors…etc.,"* Many precious masterpieces were presented to me, with a proud announcement, *"It's you grandma!"* With the months passing and the years hurrying by, I began to see great improvement in their art work. Now their masterpieces are plainly distinguishable. Complimenting a child will drive them to do better and grow in that talent or ability. Again I say, *"Its only elementary, my child."*

Words, Words, Words

Words, words, words, oh my, what do I hear!
Words, words, words, are they from you my dear?

Words, words, words, oh my, what do I feel!
Words, words, words, my heart did it steal?

Words, words, words, oh my, what do I see!
Words, words, words, have you become me?
-Mae

Throughout the many years, *words* have come and gone and transformed, destroyed and changed lives. Words will be here today, tomorrow and forever. Things might be new to us, but if time could talk, we'd understand that life just repeats itself in reference to what we do, say or even think. There is nothing new under the sun!

"That which has been is now; and that which is to be has already been"
(Ecclesiastes 1:10 NIV).

Have you ever said, *"Been there, done that?"* Truthfully, life as history, can confess this. Though we might not remember if things have been done or said before, doesn't change the fact that they have. Every generation thinks and takes ownership to sayings. The only thing new under the sun is each one of us.

In closing, if you have an elderly friend, sit and listen to them. Their stories of times past portray feelings, emotions, hurts, inner needs, and even drive. The years and times might be in distant difference, but their values, morals, principles and priorities were their foundation in striving to survive in their families.

"To live in hearts we leave behind, is not to die."
-Thomas Campbell

Plan

"Plan your work and work your plan." What a treasure in a nut shell. To have a "plan" is to have a method, an aim, a goal, a scheme or even a formula for achieving or doing something. To have a "goal" is to have a purpose or an objective for achieving or doing something. To have a "vision" is to see oneself achieving or doing that something otherwise than by the ordinary organs of sight. These three: *plan, goal* and *vision,* together equal *purpose.* "Purpose" is that which is set up as an object or end to be attained. Each and every one of us was created to have purpose. We must activate and utilize our talents, abilities, and skills to achieve our purpose in life. *"Ammunition"* is what Dad calls talents, abilities and skills, *"and your faith is what will trigger them off."* Not only ability (physical or mental power to perform), but availability (being accessible for use) is what will help us attain our purpose. All the ability in the world is no good unless it is moving.

First, ask yourself, do you know what you're worth to the world? And secondly, do you have a plan?

A plan starts with a thought, doing things in the mind before accomplishing them in reality. Although having the right intentions, but without the right plan there's no success.

Perhaps the hardest, yet the most rewarding thing for mankind to do, is to stick to their plans and goals. Working our plan through our goals develops purpose. At some point our purpose will reveal a vision for us to accomplish. Vision is the big picture where our purpose is used to achieve something big. No matter what kind of obstacles get in the way, our vision is based on what is in us. Do we really know what kind of power we have within us, *power* to ignite our vision? Do we even know what kind of authority we have within us, the kind required to carry out our vision? What about our passions, our desires and our values? We should know by now that within each one of us is a real treasure for the future.

We are to write our vision and make it plain so when we all read it, we can all run with it together. We must learn to wait on it, because it surely will come. We need to teach our children about having a plan, a goal, and a vision. When this is understood, their purpose will start to reveal itself. Once a vision is captured, it has the capability to outrun *us* into our children's generation. If this happens, *they* will continue to run with it, because it was written and plainly understood.

How many of us have already planned out our entire lives? Probably none of us, but hopefully some of us have planned out portions of it, in respect to going to college, getting married, adding a new addition to the family, a new job or career or even moving. In most life decisions, finances become a method of achieving these stages in our lives. But, and that's a strong but, what about the rest of our life? The question is not how to live *out* the rest of our days, but how to live *in* the rest of our days. We have to make our days count. Our words are a valuable source and tool in helping us plan out our lives. Remember, our words determine where we're going.

You're either in or you're out!" We've all heard this time and time again. When our middle son played football, there were times when we would see him sitting on the bench. Now, I know all parents would rather see their child out on the field looking good or blending in with the rest of the team, right? The worst was when we would see him so exhausted from working out with the rest of the team during the week after school, and still seeing him on the bench more than we hoped for. Every proud parent desires to point out their child out in the field, not on the bench. At times, I thought of asking the coach whether my son was *in* or *out*, which to us it seemed as if he was *out* most of the time, but after seeing our son happy as ever, enjoying the game, and cheering on his team-mates, it was obvious that he was "*in*". He might not have been out catching or kicking the ball, but he was supporting his team and bonding with those around him. Just because we don't see our children involved 100%, doesn't mean they aren't. Even though the plan and goal for this team was to play football, our son had captured the vision, and was doing his part in working out the plan. Sometimes it is not what others see, or even what we see, but what is being done to achieve something.

"Achievement" is successful action. Success is not just doing something. Success is achieving something. Our children's stepping stones towards life will not always be easy—for them or for us. It's not uncommon for them to want to give up half way into something. Children, as well as adults, struggle with decisions and crossroads in life, but focusing on the fact that life isn't just about *us,* helps us realize that others might need us, whether now or later.

When our son was going to Graphic/Media Arts School, at one point he wanted to drop a class (which was already paid for), because he felt it wasn't beneficial to him. When sharing this with me, I was able to remind him that maybe taking this class wasn't so much for him, but for someone else. To make a long story short, he continued with the class. Along the course of time, he was able to help and tutor other students. Even the professors appreciated his help. Being passionate about ones goals helps other's with theirs.

I was reminded of a friend I knew in High School who played football. He was sent to the bench quite often and befriended one other boy that was teased for holding the record as a bench warmer. Since the boy didn't have a father, my friend played football with him whenever possible and in return the boy tutored my friend so to keep his grades up and stay on the team. They became best of friends, and I wouldn't be surprised if they played football all through college. What my son and this friend had in common was they both were really living, making the best with every moment at hand. Now, *that* is team work.

At age five, my daughter discovered that when she gave away things to other people, she always received something in return. Seeing that her little neighbor friend didn't have nice clothes like herself, she went into her closet one day and picked out several of her nice Sunday dresses. Understanding her compassion, I allowed her to give from her best, to her best friend. Later that week, visiting my friend, who told me that her mother-in-law buys her little girl so many clothes, and many times her daughter outgrows them before she has a chance to wear them. She asked if I would like to take some of her daughter's new dresses, that didn't fit her, for my daughter. This discovery has been well practiced to this day, and passed down to our most generous grandchildren. Material things are no different in multiplying than our own words. It is of great importance for us to understand; *"What we sow, we shall reap."*

Albert M. Wells, Jr. said, *"Sharing from what we have is more important than what we have."* Sowing our time, talent and finances is more important than having time, talent and finances. It's like a river, if it's flowing it's alive, but if not, it can get stale and dry up.

Me, myself, and I. *"What a crock of beans,"* Dad would say to this remark. Remember, we are not an island to ourselves and life doesn't revolve around us. We need to look around and stay with our team. In life, other teams might come against us, but if we work together, even our children can be the great ones of their team, whether sitting or running. As often as we could, our family would meet up at a park and play softball. My dad always said he had his very own softball team—his sons and daughters. Even as family members, we stuck together, and finished what we started, we never abandoned our team in mid stream. Life needs teams of people to usher the future in with and for our children. We have a great responsibility and a great part in making this life worthwhile. This life needs us to survive. The sure way to outlive our children is by the words we leave behind for them to move forward.

"There is only one corner of the universe you can be certain of improving, and that is your own self."
–ALDOUS HUXLEY

Purpose

"The great and glorious masterpiece of man is to know how to live to purpose."
-MONTAIGNE

Earlier we learned that "Purpose" is that which is set before as an object to be reached or accomplished or the object toward which one strives for. It is our aim in life. As you read this section, you will find that it is a bit stronger and in depth deals with a greater purpose within you than you'll ever imagine. This will prepare you for the last chapter of this book, which deals with "love." I sincerely believe you are ready to move on. I do hope you will receive understanding as you read and meditate on what I want to share with you.

We were created *on purpose,* which means, not by chance nor by accident, but intentionally and deliberately. It's not to say that our parents didn't have purpose on their mind when we were conceived, but God did. There's times when I've wondered, *"What in heaven's name was God thinking when He created me?"* If God created me intentionally and deliberately, then God must have had a very wonderful plan for me. It's like us making or creating something intentionally for someone special. There's always a reason or purpose for doing what we do. Remember, when we were little, and we did something wrong? When our parents asked, *"Why in the world did you do that?"* Most kids would answer, *"I don't know."* If you think about it, whether done with good or bad intentions, there is still purpose for doing anything. We are not robots or machines doing things without a reason. If we examine any action done or even a word spoken, we will discover the motive behind it. The child doing what is wrong, might be looking for more attention. The spills in the kitchen or garage could have been a vague beginning of a project for someone. The silent tears could have been set off by loneliness. A word spoken in anger may be hiding a hurt. There is so much we can't see or hear from our children or love ones, but if we stop for a moment and remember that we are not here for only ourselves, we might discover that *on purpose* we can be part of someone else's life.

God created us *on purpose* to be part of a bigger picture. "Purpose" was what was on *His* mind, when he made each one of us. Unlike our parents, God planned out our life from birth to death. Therefore, He knows what it will take for us to live it out to completion. If our entire life was a best seller book, written and illustrated by God, wouldn't we want to live it? Surely we would read, and re-read the book over and over again to make sure we wouldn't miss a thing. What I've learned and heard over and over again, and as a matter of fact, I still hear it today; *"God is a Good God, He Loves Me, and He Wants to Bless Me."* The way I see it, is that in my own life there are blessings to be had. If it is true that God loves us, then He must have planned a great life before us complete with blessings for everyday. Now, this brings us back to, *we were created with purpose.*

How many of us really know our true purpose in life? As life continues to unveil itself before us, we will see, know and recognize our own purpose. Even in the variety of how we live our lives, whether through stepping stones to greater heights or downfalls, we must live it to its fullest. We mustn't give up. As it's been said before, "*dust yourself off and keep on going.*" Children should know that life isn't always going to be easy, but it's their life and they should make the best of it.

I'm sure you've heard this question before, *"If you knew that whatever you did, would be a success, what would you do differently?"* What a thing to think about, especially when one is on the peak time of motivation. The same goes for our children. Motivation, and praise together with encouragement will help them to believe in themselves to accomplish great things in life. Through the use of the right words and positive examples, parents can teach their children how to be successful. As a matter of fact, children start out not knowing how to fail. Does that mean that failure was taught? When a child falls, when trying to learn to walk, does he/she take it as failing or as a trying phase towards their walking phase? When we understand that within our stepping stones of greatness we will have *trying phases*, then we can assure ourselves that our falls are not fatal as long as we're moving into greatness. If you feel within to do something that seems to be a good idea, don't let anyone talk you out of it, especially yourself. Believe in yourself! Take a good long look at yourself. Now ask yourself again, "*What would I do differently, if I knew that no matter what I did, I would succeed?*" Would you be a better person? Would you be a greater person? Would you be a different person? This is a good thought to ponder for a while.

If the wisdom of good advice or golden nuggets of our past could pay for our future, would we not want to know how to take advantage of it? Of course we would, right? Well, life is like that.

"Nothing contributes so much to tranquilize the mind as a steady purpose – a point on which the soul may fix its intellectual eye."–Mary Shelly

"Purpose" is always positioned with *high aim*. Some may say to aim low, for in case you don't get what you're expecting, you won't be disappointed. My dad would call that pathetic! Again, I could hear my dad say, *"You get what you aim for."* This is what Ernest Holmes had to say about aim: *"Not failure, but low aim is a crime."* My father challenged us kids more than we wanted to be. Dad never accepted our "*not doing*" or "*not wanting to do something*" because we thought we couldn't. He either called it poor aim or low aim. "*How do you know if you cannot do it, if you haven't tried?*" was his well known reply. *"You'll never know until you try."* Many of us just need someone to stir up confidence in us; so we can aim for the best in life. Parents may have to be the confidence their children need to aim for greatness.

Everyone has space here on earth, and the "freedom" to make something of their lives. Our lives include those we love and care for. Our life is a bag of seeds. Take advantage of your space and the freedom you have to speak into others' lives. No matter how big planet earth is, there are places and people that only you and I can reach. All through this book, I have mentioned the importance of our part in touching lives in various ways. When my children were infants and they cried for specifically one or the other parent, one parent went to the rescue, only to find out that he/she wasn't the one that was requested through all the wailing. Once the right parent made his/her appeared, all was well. Sometimes life is that way. The world is crying out for someone to step up to the plate and do, or say what only that one person can do, or say. This is one way purpose is found. We might not always *do* the right things, but we should always try to *do* things right and teach our children to do so as well. Now, let's replace the "*do*" word with "*say*"; We might not always *say* the right things, but we should always try to *say* things right. These are the morals and principles we should teach our children.

My dad's most precious words to me, *"Whatever you do, if it's worth it, it's worth doing well."* Since then, I've come across similar quotes; *"Whatever you do, do with all your might."*-Cicero, and, "*Whatever your hand finds to do, do it with all your might*" (Ecclesiastes

9:*10 NIV*). These very words have been repeated throughout history for one reason only—to accomplish purpose.

Our "choices" in life are the keys and the driving force to fulfilling our purpose here on planet earth. This is called *freewill*. Our *words* are paving the road, the paths and our direction towards reaching our purpose. Our *faith* is the fuel to get us there. Much has to be considered in knowing that our words can also alter our travels. Speaking positive, believing in who we are, staying focused, and taking control of our words and actions daily, can become a lifestyle. In doing this, we can learn to discern the best, or correct path to take, when it comes to making major decisions. For example, in making our choices, whether right or wrong, doors will still open and we will be driven and excited to enter into another stage of our life, but you must examine your heart first before moving forward. At some point, if we've made the wrong choice, we'll come upon an obstacle that is totally out of order. Obstacles will always confront us no matter what, but I know that God would not open a door that we could not enter in. It is important to not want or do something because someone else is doing it. This goes for our children as well. They have their own plan in life to fulfill purpose, which may very well take them through opposite paths than their parents or brothers and sisters. Our journey into fulfilling purpose in life has only one seat; which is for the driver. Though we all have *freewill* in choosing for ourselves, careful that in choosing, you have a clear view of your vision or dream. Even in this type of lifestyle, our little ones are watching us. In your example of living wisely, you are actually sowing seed into the lives of your children.

What is "faith?" It is the confident assurance that something we want is going to happen. It is the certainty that what we hope for is waiting for us, even though we cannot see it up ahead. It is more like a position of *ultimate thinking*, which is the *final* position! Therefore, it is an action word! Faith is not a warm feeling, a cozy electrifying sensation or an emotion. As we speak words in faith, we should anticipate great things to happen, even though we don't see them now. To draw a conclusion, we understand that by faith, we have the right to speak words that we believe to be right for our life *now* and for our *future.* We also have the right to choose and believe the best for our children. Let's use our rights carefully and wisely.

"A right is not what someone gives you; it's what no one can take from you." -RAMSEY CLARK

All children are born with purpose to fulfill in their lives, and they need us to help them along the way. Wouldn't it be nice if we could see our children's lives laid out before us? What if we could peek into their future and see how they turned out. If this was possible, don't you think it would change the way we deal with them or the way we talk to them today? Well, just believing that our children were created to be special and accomplish great things in life is enough for us to want to see them succeed. Our faith in them will trickle down to their very being and they, too, will begin to see and believe that they were born to have an amazing life. With our words we can begin to speak and confess before them their successful future. These are Mr. Kelly's words:

"Each of us can live such a life of amazing power and peace and serenity...on one condition – that is, if we really want to."
-THOMAS KELLY

CHAPTER SIX

Love

Lifestyle

"Lifestyle" is a way of life that reflects an individual's preference or value. It would be nice if life came with such instructions as, "Now that you have a *life*, choose a *style* for it, and live everyday by your *preferences* until they become of *value*" Or perhaps, "Your *life* automatically comes with a thing called *LOVE*, apply it according to your preferences until your *Life* becomes *VALUABLE*, then enjoy high doses daily." In reality, we do have to make choices as to what kind of life we want to lead our family into. The right preferences used in the building of a healthy lifestyle for you and your family is priceless.

Many of you believe as I do, that love comes with every life given to mankind. Love may very well lie dormant deep in the heart of men and women, and children; having not been activated. Perhaps, one reason being; not everyone knows what love is. I believe there are few people who know what *real love* is, fewer who have actually experienced *real love,* but the good news is, we have all been *loved!*

Sayings such as; *"Love makes the world go 'round"*, *"Love covers all sin"*, *"Love conquers all"*, and *"Love is the greatest of all human qualities"*, have made their way to our ears over and over in our own lifetime. Not everyone will agree with these, but I will take the liberty to clear up a few things in my own understanding that might help someone out.

No greater love here on earth can compare to the love of a mother for her child. We have all seen, or witnessed, how a mother's love is expressed in many ways, styles and fashions. There's even the love that can't be expressed, not to say it isn't love. People have funny ways of expressing love, depending on what they love. After reading this chapter, you will want to examine your love for others.

Shortly after I had my first child, I attended a Mother's Day Banquet. All mothers, who attended, received a copy of the "Recipe of Love" in a beautiful silver frame. Though I was young, I knew in order for this recipe to have significance, it had to be applied. As cute as this poem may seem, keep in mind that love can only be measured by our hearts. Without any of the following ingredients, it is impossible to have love. Think of each ingredient as a seed, the more you sow, the more you'll reap. Feel free to share your recipe of love daily with those around and about you.

RECIPE of LOVE

1 large quantity of Love
2 fractions of Trust
4 portions of Faith
3 parts of Understanding
2 helpings of Tenderness
2 sections of Kindness
4 morsels of Friendship
5 servings of Hope
4 fragments of Forgiveness
1 unit of Laughter

Take ***Love*** *and* ***Trust*** *and mix it thoroughly with* ***Faith****. Blend it with* ***Understanding, Tenderness*** *and* ***Kindness****. Add* ***Friendship*** *and* ***Hope.*** *Bake it in the Sunshine.*

Next spread ***Forgiveness*** *all over and sprinkle abundantly with colorful* ***Laughter****. Serve generous amounts daily.*

Throughout the years, I have seen these types of keys surface time and time again in reference to marriages, raising children, friendships and even in celebrating Mothers on Mother's Day. It would be wise to take a deeper look into what the message is really about. However anyone chooses to apply these golden nuggets is their option, but I know, for a fact, that none of these ingredients can have their full affect on anyone without personally applying the spoken word. Try speaking the ingredients into someone's life.

If we had a choice, wouldn't we prefer hearing "I love you" versus a written note alone on letters or cards received, especially from our love ones? It's a natural thing to want the person giving us the card to read what they've written to us. Even when a card is store-bought and selected especially for us, it has so much more life in it when we hear the words being read out loud. Am I right? Of course I am. Remember, a word is an action ready to be activated by speech.

In 1952 Alexander McQueen wrote, *"On almost every page of a dictionary are clues to the origin and development of our language. Such clues may be traced from mankind's earliest days – through the ancient civilizations of Greece and Rome – and into modern period, where, with the piling up of new discoveries in the arts and sciences, the invention of new words has become almost common. Every word we use has a history, and in almost every case it is a story of action – a story of something happening. The word forming activity has been going on for thousands of years, ever since the first human beings uttered the first human sounds. We have inherited a rich legacy."* So every word has a story of action, a story of something happening. How interesting.

Have you ever heard the word, "love-style?" Neither had I, until I made it up for this chapter. I think I'm allowed to make up a word that will fit my style of writing. Well, I'll just call it *my* word, since I've learned something from it. The way I see it, if "lifestyle" *is a way of life that reflects an individual's preferences or values*, then it would be a fitting definition if I tweaked it a bit to fit "love-style." Imagine the definition to be; *a way or manner of love that reflects an individual's preferences or values.* Cool definition, huh? A "lifestyle" a way of life, and "love-style" a way of love should take precedence in most homes naturally as we take great pride in educating our children. The question is; does our *Love* reflect our children's value?

"Style" is the individuality that is expressed in a person's actions and tastes. Everyone has their own style of living and loving. I personally like to express love through my actions. This kind of love that enables me to care for others and try to help them in how ever I can, is a lifestyle developed in my character from childhood.

Not every person knows what real love is, and some are even convinced they are in love, when they're not. Many people don't even discover true love until many years after marriage. At the end of this book you will discover what real "Love" is, and how it should be lived as. Once "love" has been fully defined in your life you will feel richer for knowing and energized within to want to have a love-style type of life daily.

The home should be the school for love. Examples of love are seen through our family members, relatives and friends that are dear to us. Here I am referring to the type of love that is general and the bases for all levels of love. I came from a large family of eleven kids. Now, at this point you might be thinking to yourself, *"Now, there was a lot of love in that house!"* You are absolutely right. My parents birthed a home full of love. The same values, principles and morals I learned at home, whether through example or a lifestyle made me who I am today. I am not saying that I had the perfect family, which there isn't such a family, but I do know that love was poured into each of us equally, with an understanding that Mom and Dad only wanted the best for each one of us. I knew this value—I felt it, and I saw it. Whether rebellion, stubbornness or simple laziness appeared around the clock at different stages, I was still aware of being loved and cared for. In our home, there was always enough love to go around, no one felt more loved than the other. Mom and Dad's circle of love embraced all eleven of us together.

In my Sunday school years, I learned that "God *is* Love." I didn't understand this concept then, but today I understand it to mean that if God *is* Love and God *always was*, then love was not created—but has always been. If God *is* Love, then we were created by Love. Now, since God *is in Love* with us, then we were created in Love. It was *through His Love* and *with His Love* that we were created. For those who want to know the foundation of this quote, read Genesis 1:26-27. "*We are created in the image of Love*". Consequently, if we were created *by Love, in Love, with Love*, and *through Love*, then we definitely have all been "Loved."

"Love is the outgoing force of the soul, the God-in-man."
-FRANCOIS DE LA ROCHEFOUCAULD

The easiest lessons, instructions, teachings, and coaching on love is taught by example and lifestyle. I've seen an infant in love with its baby doll or stuff animal, hugging and holding tightly to it. It is apparent that they are expressing the first stages of love. Have you ever wondered how they know this? Could it be that love was in them from birth? Or at what stage of their young life did they perceive the action of love given to them? How was it that they knew how to express love?

"The best and most beautiful things in the world cannot be seen or even touched; they must be felt with the heart."

Helen Keller's wise words above can surely define love as one of those beautiful things in the world. This would be an excellent answer for any teen that asks, *"When will I know when I'm in-love?"*

Our duty as parents and guardians makes us
do things well, but as Zig Ziglar says it:

"LOVE makes us do things beautifully."

Have you ever heard, *owe nothing but love?* Owing "love" sounds like a debt to me, a nice kind of debt to have. Reading an interesting verse, made me realize how important Love really is. *"Pay all your debts except the debt of love for others – never finish paying that" (Romans 13:6 LV).* It is easier to understand the previous chapters with this one golden nugget. We are to *love* one another, keep on *loving* our neighbors, speak the truth in *love*, be rooted and grounded in *love* and walk in *love* all the days of our life. Because *love* has no end, it will not die nor go away. *Love* is in us and if nurtured it will keep on growing from one generation to another. We've all heard people say, *"You've got your mother's love; she loved everyone."* Or maybe something like this, *"You've got your Dad's heart, always loving and helping people."* When we pour our best into our children, whether through words or actions, we are sowing the finest seeds for the future.

"To love abundantly is to live abundantly, and to love forever is to live forever."
-ALPHONSE MARIE LOUIS DE LAMARTINE

As one famous author wrote, *"May your roots go down deep into the soil of God's marvelous Love, and may you be able to understand how long, how wide, how deep, and how high His Love really is; and to experience this Love for yourselves, though it is so great that you will never see the end of it or fully know or understand it. And so at last, you will be filled up with God himself" (Ephesians 3:17-19 LV).*

Wow! That is some kind of LOVE! This kind of *love* reaches every corner of our experience. It is long; it continues the length of our lives. It is deep; it reaches to the depth of discouragement, despair, and even death. It is wide; it covers the breadth of our own life, and reaches out to the whole world. It is high; it rises to the heights of our celebration. God's love is expressed in such detail and greatness so we will feel totally secure. Just knowing that God's love is forever and nothing can separate us from something eternal, is enough motivation to help us all express our deep love for our love ones. Just imagine how secure our children would be, knowing the depth of our love for them. Speak it to them.

Value

A child, a gift to us, is born so pure. As they grow up, there's no fear in them trying anything new. By observing other life activity around them they make every effort to fit in. Seeing a child develop surely indicates that they believe they can. We are all born with those same qualities and values, but once we begin to change and developed, we oftentimes stop believing in ourselves, turning to the world around us as our mentor. The world cannot tell us how to live our lives, rear our children, or develop into someone that we were not created to be. If we stop looking at the world, and mind our own business, we will find that there will always be someone to guide us and help us along our path in life. In most cases, the primary guiding begins at home for our own children. Love starts with us. Love enhances our value as a person. Read on to see what magnificent beings we are created to be. The most important thing we must know, and pass down to our children is that;

"No one can make you feel inferior without your consent."
–ELEANOR ROOSEVELT

We are a masterpiece, one of a kind, and our rarity gives us value. We should continually sow a seed of reassurance in our children, so they, too, will know without a doubt, that *they are priceless.*

Since every word and action is a seed sown, knowingly or not, it will sprout after its kind. What are we teaching our children at home, at school and in the street? Good seeds give good fruit. Everything we do, we must do with *love.* It's a good thing to develop a style of love in teaching, talking and doing what we do best, being ourselves around our children. If we rehearse to our children that no one can be them, only them, they will grasp the fact that they are the best "them" in existence. Being an original is being one of a kind!

Our children will at some point witness some unfortunate circumstances along their journey in life. As parents and guardians, we should be careful to not express personal or inappropriate guidance to such situations. Let me share a short story about a six year old with a strong foundation.

Neighborhood thieves found it amusing to enter a garage in the middle of the night. The following morning, the discovery of missing things from the vehicles in the garage was a shock to the children. As the mom explained the situation and assured them that everything was going to be all right, they eventually calmed down. Their mom went on to seal mental security in them by adding, *"Honey, we have to share this world with people who don't know any better, and because of their actions, they end up hurting others over and over again. Some people have hatred in their hearts, thus causing them to do wrong things, but we can't hate them."*

The six year old jumped up, *"I learned in school that we should pray for those who hurt us. So I will pray for that person."* Now, I wonder how many people take the time to pray for thieves nowadays. It took a calm, faithful, and strong woman to teach *love* and not allow *hate* into her children's thinking. This kind of guidance helps a child know himself and builds a strong foundation, no matter what comes along in their life.

We are not called *parents* or *guardians* for the sake of just holding a title. Mothers, Fathers and Guardians are all caregivers. We defend and protect the ones we love and no one can do it better. No machine, no computer, no organization can give to our own flesh and blood what we were entrusted to give them; ourselves. Sir Lancelot says it best;

"The gift without the giver is bare. The only true gift is a portion of one's self."

Since I mentioned computers, let me put in my two bits of info that might stir up your thinking. Many men of the past had dreams of the day when computers will be so far ahead of human intelligence that we would be second best. In 1950 they believed that a computer would be able to translate perfectly from one language to another. Now, today they are saying that neither of these things has happened. One problem with machine translations is that computers do exactly what one tells them to do, no more, no less. I read once that the human language is rich in images and shades of meaning that a computer cannot handle. Human language uses the senses of our inner and outer being. That's why we call it action in motion. The difference is that computer language is a mathematical language. Numbers are a human invention. Though clear and precise in numbers, there are plenty of things in the real world that computers cannot describe or interpret—like love.

Imagine there being an attempt to build a machine in the image of man, but to do this it appears necessary to see man in the image of a machine. As Malcolm E. Weiss put it, *"This seems to be a dangerous vision."* He goes on to clarify, *"the true moral of the Zulu tale is not that robots took over the world because they were superior to man. It was that people turned over their responsibilities to machines because they believed the machines were superior."* Humans believed that machines were superior? Wow!

If computers had ears, two for that matter, they would have the capacity to store more information than can be stored in dozens of their most sophisticated models. If computers had a mind, they could store more information than man will find in the millions of volumes in any library. So to create a human brain, it would probably cost billions of dollars, plus it's estimated that it would be larger than the Empire State Building, not to mention the use of more electricity than a city of a thousand people use today. If brilliant men could build something as such, this man-made brain couldn't originate a single thought, which a real live human can do in a blink of an eye. What an amazing creation we are!

Computers don't have the seventy-two muscles, as man, that work in perfect coordination each time he utters a single word. Now, who is superior? Besides, there is absolutely no style of love in how computers relate to us. Humans are valuable beings who create valuable machines, not the other way around.

We have a great responsibility to our children and no one is superior over our children, but God and us.

Don't we feel better when we're all squeaky clean and dressed up? What works for adults, also works for kids. Outward appearance does affect our performance, either enhancing or crippling the potential within. It is very importance to teach our children to take care of themselves physically. Starting them young, in caring how they look, sooner or later they will take charge, all on their own. A good seed to sow in them daily is complimenting them on how nice they look, or smell after a good clean-up. This nugget is vital to being all they are created to be. We must do our part in helping develop simple, yet healthy values in our children by promoting self-acceptance. It's important to fill our children's treasure with words that encourage and build them up through every stage of their lives, even the difficult years. The seeds we sow in their lives can get them through tough times. The better they look, the better they'll feel about themselves.

Our world is filled and overflowing with great men and women who can inspire us with their lives of success. We can assure ourselves that success didn't fall out of the sky, or pop up at their first try, and neither will it for us. Failure shows up quit frequently when success is around the corner. We were not designed to be failures. We were designed to overcome failures no matter how often they come knocking! Failure doesn't mean fatal. We can call it anything else, whether we choose to see them as stepping stones to success, learning stages of success, or opportunities for improvement, either way it leads to some kind of success. Don't quit!

"If you don't succeed the first time, try, try, and try again."

To "try again" is the secret to success. We can learn from the successful failures of many people. There are people most often mentioned in reference to their failures before their great success such as, Abraham Lincoln, Thomas Edison, Albert Einstein, and even Walt Disney himself. Take time to look up these men and many more on the Web and be encouraged. Life is the trial, Living is the success. Make the best of your living for you and your children. Be sure to speak life into your child's future by complimenting him in the present.

Most of us have succeeded in various things in our lives, so have our children. There are many levels of success, especially in children. Acknowledge each level of their success; being there to help them reach their next level, whether physically, materially, socially, or spiritually. Make it clear to your children that failure is not fatal and teach them how to stay true to their goals.

"It is impossible to influence someone else for the good and give them a boost or a compliment without gaining a benefit yourself."

"A sincere compliment is one of the most effective teaching and motivational methods in existence."

We must be selective in who or what our children listen to. Remember, in the earlier chapters, we read that what we hear also influences us and our children? Our hearing should consist only of good and healthy words that builds us up, encourages, teaches and enhances values of our lifestyle.

My dad would say, *"Give me something worth listening to."* To him words were of an essence and worth his time, so it was vital that whoever was doing the talking was dishing out something of value for my dad to find worth listening to. Even as teenagers when we got caught in a predicament, which was difficult to explain, he still wanted to hear words of worth instead of a lot of jibber jabber. Make your words to those around you worth the message it is delivering.

It is just as important to be a "good listener." *"Talking is sharing but listening is caring."* Listening to the myriads of detail and small talk in a child's day, demonstrates that we care and it sets the stage for them to learn by our actions. Teaching our children to talk with value will make them good listeners.

Everlasting

Love is not an emotion, it is an action, *Love* is not a feeling, it is an experience and *Love* is not earned, it is free. The best part of all—*Love is forever*! *Love* will outlive everything here on earth. As Williams James puts it;

"The greatest use of life is to spend it on something that will outlast it."

It is safe to say, *Love* should be worth its spending, especially if it becomes a lifestyle. It is quite possible that most of us would want to learn more on how to spend (sow) our love; so it will outlast our own lives as it *streams* over into our children's lives.

"Stream" reminds me of a river. A river is always active, streaming up or streaming down. If it stops streaming there's a chance of it getting polluted or contaminated. Have you ever seen a dried up river or stream? It loses its purity and clarity, becoming dirty, filthy, and even smelly. Its style of living expired. *Love* keeps our lifestyle active with our words: words worth outlasting life.

Weddings and anniversaries are perfect settings for *Love* to be expressed in the most beautiful ways. It is most common to see "Love" quoted from what is known as the "Love Chapter" in I Corinthians 13. It is here where *Love* is identified in the most unique and graceful way, capturing the value of what LOVE truly is. I like to begin with vs.4-6, *"Love is very patient and kind, never jealous or envious, never boastful or proud, never haughty or selfish or rude. Love does not demand its own way. It is not irritable or touchy. It does not hold grudges and will hardly even notice when others do it wrong. It is never glad about injustice, but rejoices whenever truth wins out."*

Verses 1-3 challenges us, *"If I had the gift of being able to speak in other languages without learning them, and could speak in every language there is in all of heaven and earth, but didn't Love others, I would only be making noise. If I had the gift of prophecy and knew all about what is going to happen in the future, knew everything about everything, but didn't Love others, what good would it do? Even if I had the gift of faith so that I could speak to a mountain and make it move, I would still be worth nothing at all without Love. If I gave everything to the poor people, and if I were burned alive for preaching the Gospel but didn't Love others, it would be of no value whatever."* *("no value whatever" translates as: it profits me nothing or I gain nothing.)

Next, v.7, is Love's duty offered to us, *"If you Love someone you will be loyal to him* (or her) *no matter what the cost. You will always believe in him* (or her), *always expect the best of him* (or her), *and always stand your ground in defending him* (or her).

Verse 8 finalizes it with, *"...Love goes on forever."* Love never fails!

In this chapter, I enjoyed capitalizing the word "Love", because I understand that God is Love and Love is God; so when I read the "Love" chapter (God's chapter), it becomes breathtaking when I insert "God" everywhere I read "Love." I challenge you to read it for yourself and experience a new revelation of "Love" that you've not known before. For a regular reminder of what true Love is, try reading the "Love chapter" daily.

Similar to the *Recipe of Love* mentioned earlier, here the author points out several specifics of love, which are patience, kindness, generosity, humility, courtesy, unselfishness, good temper, and sincerity. These expressions communicate clearly the love from one human to another. This is true heavenly love on earth.

Once I read a story of a young couple who received a very special card from a friend on their wedding day. The text in the card was from the "Love Chapter." The instructions on the card were: "Fill in the blanks with 'LOVE.'" This is what the card looked like; "_____ *is very patient and kind, never jealous or envious, never boastful or proud, never haughty or selfish or rude. _____ does not demand its own way. _____ is not irritable or touchy. _____ does not hold grudges and will hardly even notice when others do it wrong."* At that precious moment, the only thought of LOVE on the bride's mind, was her sweet husband; so she lovingly filled in *his* name in the blanks. Many years later she found the same card in an old shoe box in the attic. On their 50th anniversary, she resealed it in a new envelope and gave it to her husband. It was obvious that after 50 years, true Love was the strong foundation of their marriage.

Love abides in us and can be seen only through our actions and the influence we have on others. Love fits all sizes and shapes, all walks of life and all personalities, whether young or old. Love is easier to describe than to define, it is a word most misunderstood in the English language today. Love is confused with physical attraction, lust, personal desire, sympathy and compassion. Yet, Love is one of the most common experiences of mankind. Webster defines "love" as a feeling of strong personal attachment *induced* by feeling, or by ties of kinship or affection.

Although "Love" lasts forever, it only acts in the present. Many refer to it as a gift, freshly given to us every day. No one can love anything or anyone yesterday, nor tomorrow, only today. Love should be our aim daily. Love is eternal because of the seeds sown in the past, present and future. At the end of this book, you will learn that the greatest Seed ever to be sown was for us.

"Love is a thing that's never out of season."
-BARRY CORNWALL

In wrapping up this final chapter with the most meaningful nuggets on "True Love" that you'll ever encounter in your life, I do hope they will serve you well. As that inner spark of love within begins to grow, you will desire more. With love; the more we give, the more we get. The following three Golden Nuggets are the strongest base on which one can build a strong family foundation on: *First, we must honestly love God and trust him with all our life. Secondly, we must honestly love ourselves. Thirdly, we must honestly love our neighbors as ourselves.* These things might be difficult at times, but in order to do our part in changing the world through the words we speak, there has to be *love.* Then we can begin to develop a lifestyle of doing and saying everything in *love.* Love causes us to care when no one else does. Love causes us to move into action. Love never fails us and it is priceless.

***"With malice towards none, with love for all,
with firmness in the right, as God gives us to see the right,
let us strive on to finish the work we are in."***
-ABRAHAM LINCOLN

God's love for us, cannot be measured, nor compared to anyone or anything we know or will ever know. The foundation to our purpose is to *love,* and through *love* we have the keys to everything we need in life. Our lives, as well as our children's lives, are valuable to us, to others and to God. Love is not singular, it is plural. It is an action that is diverse, it multiplies, it is numerous, it has variety, it is the majority, and it can be overwhelming. I cannot say that I am here for me, myself and I. Everything within me is meant to be shared. We have seeds of greatness, which are meant to be sown, to bring a harvest, not just one plant or shoot, but a full harvest!. We have talents and abilities that can only work with others around us. And we have the power of our words as fuel into the future.

Now, how we came to be was by a word spoken. I'm not talking about Mom and Dad making plans for your beginning. I am talking about the greatest words ever spoken from the beginning of time: the eternal Words of God. These Words, still spoken today, can have the greatest influence in all of our lives.

We should all try to get our hands on what is known to most children as the *Basic Instructions Before Leaving Earth* book, best referred to as the "Bible." I like to think of it as God's book of mail to me. If God has spoken in the past, through His Word, to many men, women and yes, children, why is it any different today? Every day I like to know that, "I got mail" from above.

Since God is Love and the Bible is His book to us, then it stands to reason that anyone who reads it will be filling their heart with endless treasures. The Bible is a book of love, wisdom, direction, and guidance for all man to be equipped and live the life they were created for. This book definitely changes lives and puts in order what God's plan for mankind is. We are to *read* it, *believe* it, and *apply* it by *confessing* and *speaking* out God's Powerful Word over our lives. In the beginning God gave us an illustration of how powerful His words were: *He spoke the world into existence!* Today His Word is more powerful than you can ever imagine.

Our human abilities, our purpose and the seeds within us, are God's greatest tools to touch generation after generation. If we know and understand that our words are powerful, how much more is God's Word? *"The Word of God is living and active, sharper than any double-edged sword"* (Hebrews 4:12 NIV). I challenge you today, to begin reading the Bible. If you search God's Word with passion, I promise you it will change your life. If you have made God's Word the most powerful Words that you will ever speak over your own life and others, rest assure, there is definitely no better way to life than what God has already left us in His Word. Speaking it will activate His promises into our lives.

God's Word has infinite value.

In order to learn and mature as God desires us to, read His Word, believe it and apply it daily. Finding a Church that teaches from the Word of God (meaning directly from the Bible), and surrounding yourself with other Christians can help tremendously in your walk with the Lord.

Once again, I want to remind you, *God loves you* and He needs you to care enough to have a life worth living. He needs you to believe Him so He can become personal with you! He wants you to believe that He wants to truly bless you! He truly is a good God. He will never force you to love Him, but His love for you will never change regardless. If you believe He is love than you have taken the first step in *His* direction for your life. The ability to enjoy life is one of God's most excellent love gifts to you. A life worth living starts with a priceless treasure of love in your heart. Accepting God's Love in your heart is accepting God Himself.

"One word – frees us of all the weight and pain of life; that word is Love."
-SOPHOCLES

God foresaw that someday we would need an answer to face this difficult world. Every promise in His book comes with two choices, either we take it or not. When we believe in God, we believe everything about Him. The following words define His character, "God is a good God. God loves you. God wants to bless you." Because God is Love, He can *only* function in Love.

God had an ultimate gift for us, His finest treasure ever, His greatest Love—His Only Son, Jesus. Sending Jesus to us as a Savior and Lord of our lives was God's way of drawing us closer to Him. Receiving His gift comes with a promise that He would be with us always. God's heartbeat is for His children to have all that belongs to them. Our Father in heaven wants to send us blessings through His Son as His Spirit dwells within our heart. Our ability to believe in Him, gives us the ability to do great things for Him. With this we come to believe that *"greater is He that is in us, than he that is in the world" (1John 4:4 KJV).* If God be with us and for us, then nothing can be against us, because we have the power to overcome by the *words* of our testimony.

Jesus comes to us as the gift of eternal life, and everlasting love. God's greatest treasure for all His children is assuring a life with Him forever. If you need this kind of treasure and reassurance in your life, please confess and make the following prayer yours today, then sign and date it for your own record.

Dear God,

Thank you for loving me. Thank you for your gift of eternal life. I receive your Son Jesus as my Lord and Savior over my life and in my heart today as my finest treasure ever. Cleanse my life and fill me with your love and your peace. All that I am, I give to you, and all that you are I receive in me, today. Amen.

"Today I received Jesus Christ as my Lord and Savior."
Signed: ________________________________
Dated: ________________________________

Congratulations, you are now a child of God! I celebrate you! May God's blessings be upon you and your children. Remember, the Bible (*Basic Instructions Before Leaving Earth)* will reveal God's Love to you as the greatest treasure you will ever know. Make your greatest aim *Love* and let's make this world beautiful!!!

"By wisdom a house is built, and through understanding it is established; through knowledge its rooms are filled with rare and beautiful treasures"
(Proverbs 24:3-4 NIV).

"There is only one happiness in life, to love and be loved."
-GEORGE SAND (1862)

Dear Reader,

I have included a short prayer for you to pray every day to help you along the way to a better you for the future. Just remember, pray from your heart. Wish you the best.

With Love,
Mae

Dear God,

Thank you for loving me. Help me daily to be a better person as I become aware of the words I speak and the things I do. I want to change my life and choose a better future for me and my children. I believe that together, we can make a difference in this world, starting one day at a time. I ask all this in your son, Jesus' name. Amen.

References

- *Fruit of The Lips*-Don Hughes. Evangelistic Association.1975.
- "The Birds And The Bees"-words and music by Herb Newman.
- Mariana Valverde. Professor of Criminology.Wikipedia.org/wiki/marian-valverde
- "The Controlled Tongue"-The Living Bible. Tyndale House Publishing, Inc. 1988.
- *The Story of the Constitution*-Sol Bloom. New York.1937.
- "Wise Learners vs. Foolish Failures"-Bible. (LV). Tyndale House Publishers, Inc. 1988.
- *Our Amazing World of Nature, Its Marvels and Mysteries.* Reader's Digest. 1969.
- *Am. Legacy Our National Forests* .Kenneth Brown. Published by National Geographic Society. 1997.
- *Comforting Scents*-Valerie Gennari Cooksley. Prentice Hall Press.1998.
- *Gods, Stars And Computers Fact and Fancy in Myth and Science.* Malcolm E. Weiss Doubleday & Company, Inc. 1980.
- *See You at The Top*-Zig Ziglar. Pelican Publishing Company.1991.
- "MPAA-Children'sTelevisionStandardRatings".2005.www.mpaa.org/film.ratings.
- Research Study: "Harvard Kids at Risk Project".2003.http://Kidsrisk.harvard.edu.

- *Where to Find it in The Bible* .Ken Anderson-The A to Z Resource. Thomas Nelson Publishers.1996, 2001.
- *The New Webster's Encyclopedic Dictionary of The English Language Consolidated Book*. Published 1971.
- *The New Webster's International Encyclopedia. The New Illustrated Home Reference Guide*. Trident Press International. 1996.
- *The American Heritage Dictionary of the English Language*. American Heritage Publishing Co. Inc. and Houghton Mifflin Company.1969.
- *Webster's Ninth New Collegiate Dictionary a Merrian-Webster-Inc.*, Publisher. 1985.
- *A compendious Dictionary of The English Language*. Noah Webster. (A facsimile of 1809 edition). Bounty Books A Division Of Crown Publishers, Inc. 1970.
- *The New Collins Thesaurus*. Wllm. Collins Sons & Co. Ltd. 1984.
- *Smith's Bible Dictionary*. Barbour Publishing, Inc. 1987.
- *Parallel Bible. NIV/KJV*. Zondervan Bible Publishers. Copyright.1985.
- *Bible. The Life Application. Living Version*. Tyndale House Publishers, Inc. and Youth For Christ/USA.1988.
- *Lifetime Speaker's Encyclopedia, Volume 1 & 2*. Jacob M. Braude Prentice-Hall, Inc. 1962.

About the Author

Mae Archila, a wife of 38 years, mother of three, and grandmother of two, was born in Moorhead, Minnesota. She is the oldest daughter of eleven brothers and sisters. Mae highly values family as one of the greatest gift and blessing anyone can have. Many personal life experiences have been a pallet for her writing. Her love for children and the study of God's Word has always been the passion and motivation behind her writing and teaching. She strongly believes that whatever she learns, especially from God's Word, is meant to be shared.

Mae and her husband own and run an architecture company from their home in Boca Raton, Florida. They are both very active in their home church, loving people and growing in the things of God. Mae's greatest dream is to be used by God to reach the world with life through her writing, changing lives one word at a time.

CPSIA information can be obtained at www.ICGtesting.com
Printed in the USA
BVOW040545091211

277942BV00002B/14/P